Miquel Barceló

ACQUAVELLA

This publication accompanies the exhibition

Miquel Barceló

ON VIEW
OCTOBER 27-DECEMBER 9, 2016

Acquavella Galleries
18 East 79th Street
New York, NY 10075

Je suis d'outre-mer, je ne suis pas d'ici –
I am from overseas, I'm not from here
© 2016 Catherine Lampert

Library of Congress Control Number
2016953413

ISBN 978-0-9981156-0-3

DESIGN
Henk van Assen with Kelly Bryan
HvADESIGN, NY

PRINT
Phoenix Group, Philadelphia, PA

COVER
Kraken central, 2015
Mixed media on canvas
74 $^3/_4$ x 106 $^1/_4$ inches (190 x 270 cm)

Foreword

Eleanor Acquavella Dejoux

Acquavella Galleries is delighted to present our second exhibition of new work by Miquel Barceló, featuring two new series of paintings by the artist in addition to a selection of his recent ceramics. In these paintings, which are being exhibited for the first time, Miquel returns to two subjects that have continued to inspire him throughout his career; the vivid blue paintings evoke the Mallorcan artist's love for the sea, and the corrida pictures mark his return to his long-favored subject of the bullfight. In her poetic essay, the art historian Catherine Lampert elegantly describes the subjects and materials of these new works, contextualizing them within the artist's oeuvre and unveiling his many sources of inspiration.

In the planning of this exhibition, it has been a pleasure to work with Miquel's assistants, Victoria Comune, Jean-Philippe Fournier, and Maria Hevia, and we would also like to thank Tobias Mueller and his team at Tobias Mueller Modern Art and Bruno Bischofberger for their help in the organization of this show. At the gallery, our thanks go to Emily Crowley, Kathleen Krall, Jean Edmonson, Jennifer Rose, Garth Szwed, Eric Theriault, and Devon Vogt for their work on the exhibition. Our gratitude also goes to Henk van Assen and his team at HvADesign and Keith Harrington at Phoenix for their help in designing and printing the catalogue. Above all, we would like to thank Miquel for making these beautiful works and for working closely with the gallery on the planning of the exhibition.

Ceramics in Miquel Barceló's studio, 2016

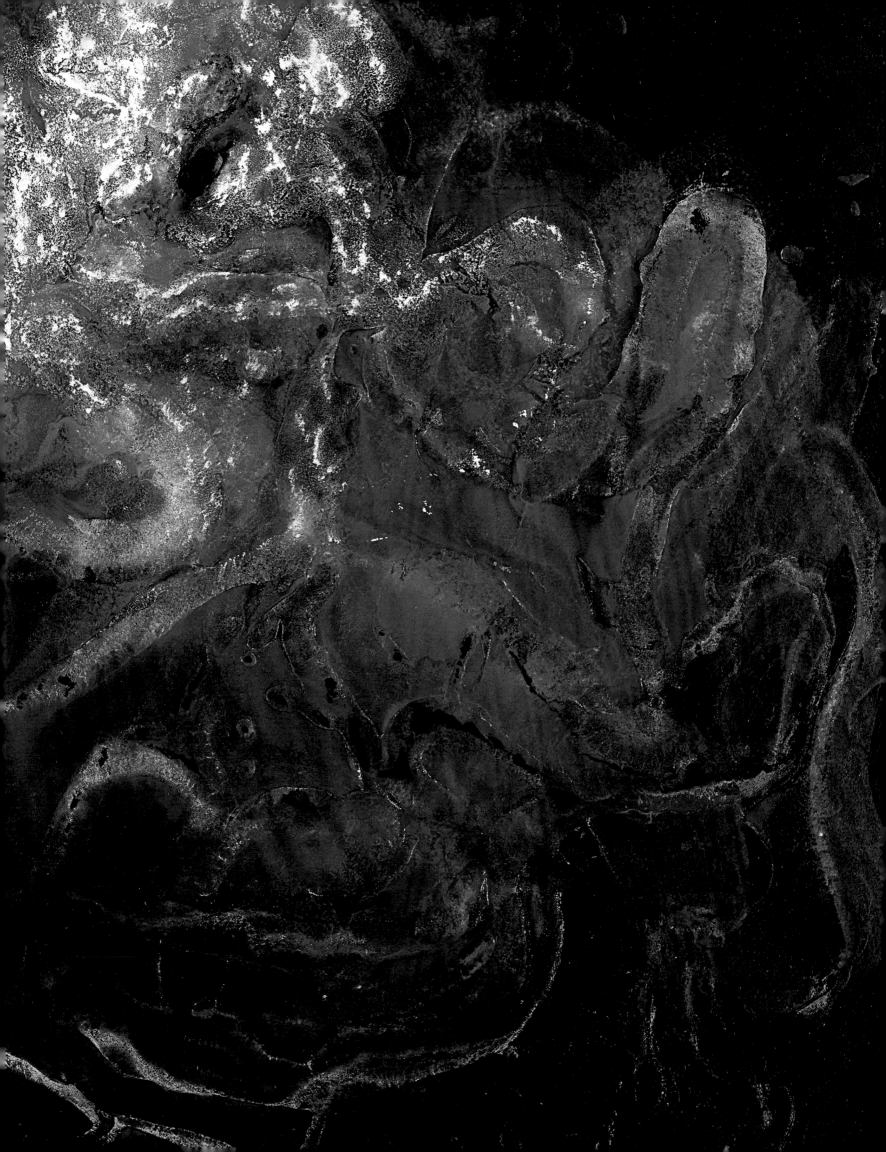

Je suis d'outre-mer, je ne suis pas d'ici—

I am from overseas, I'm not from here

Catherine Lampert

Like anyone writing this kind of essay, I try to imagine the pictures I've seen in Miquel Barceló's studios and anticipate what they will be like arranged in the refined neoclassical spaces of the Acquavella Galleries. Barceló hopes to immerse the visitor in his work the way Giotto's frescoes in the Arena Chapel in Padua still do, 700 years after they were completed. The new blue paintings, some using the same lapis lazuli known to Fra Angelico and Giotto, range in size from 60 x 80 cm to 190 x 270 cm; what would it be like if all fifteen were installed floor to ceiling? If you stand in front of one of the paintings large enough to fill the whole of one's gaze, the eye roams, as if scanning forms, coming across bursts of piercing white light, at once strangely alien and hyperrealist. Many clearly suggest species of marine life, the tentacles of an octopus reach to the edge of the rectangle and the head protrudes; an ugly brown squid, *sipiota*, in one painting and an elegant tuna in another, glide along the sea floor; and writhing unnameable varieties of larvae are suspended in the saturated pools of paint that cover these surfaces. The viewer confronts a mature torpedo-like form that radiates in multiple directions and ends in dark orifices. Splatters of black are fixed to the surface,

the subterranean flux agitated by spume, squalls, sponges, a roaring noise, a natural vortex, the swirling flow of water. In his childhood, Barceló trained himself to dive for octopus in order to emulate the twenty-year-old heroes in his hometown of Felanitx; and he continues to dive, locally and abroad (he descended fifty meters in Papua New Guinea at the beginning of 2016).

In a number of blue paintings, the dominant motif is circular. Barceló mentions the veneration of the hole and the empty pavilion in various cultures, notably the *tokonoma* in Japan which he associates with the poem, *El pabellón del vacío*, 1976, by the Cuban writer José Lezama Lima; the word appears when the narrator enters and occupies an imaginary space. One also thinks of an aureole, both the spiritual kind and that of igneous intrusions and asteroids. Another circle is the single beautiful sphere, moon-like, heavily cratered, illuminated in full or partly in shadow, for example, the suspended *Lune gibbeuse décroissante*, 2016. From the terrace of the artist's house in Cap de Farrutx, overlooking the Mediterranean, on certain days you can see the dangerous waves that originate a long distance away, moving slowly, the

FIG. 1
View from the artist's terrace in Farrutx, Mallorca

strong currents still treacherous, the cycle of the tides disturbed, the bulge in the sea governed by gravity and the planets. [FIG. 1] While still in his teens, Barceló began watching how the ecology of Mallorca was degrading, and reminds us that several species of fish (and plants) have changed in the last fifty years, a few are already extinct, and in places the coast has eroded.

In some respects, the newest pictures revisit concepts Barceló explored in his early twenties when he placed raw substances and a hand-fashioned blue pigment into glass-covered boxes. [FIG. 2] "My idea was that somewhere in the rotting process the first layers would tear away and the blue paint would become visible."[1] Today this layering and repelling is conducted with enormous inventiveness and skill, the results simulating a kind of metamorphosis that appears as if auto-generated. The grandest images eschew all illusionist marks and seem to arise from eruptions, explosions, forms pushing through from underneath, fissures. The paintings are suggestive of a loss of control, of exhilarating aerial weightlessness and vicarious sensations of plunging deep through the sea, being submerged, dreaming,

drowning; yet, the placement of masses in space and within the rectangle is the opposite of random, indeed the surface tension is enormous and precise.

Barceló reminds me that he prefers to "act" when he doesn't know what to do, when there is an explanation, or a pictorial solution leading to the realization of a work, the idea quickly becomes uninteresting. Although on the back of some canvases there are rudimentary diagrams, a spiral, an oval with one end in shadow, the real adventure begins with direct contact with the materials. Barceló derives pleasure from his large stocks of powdered pigments, most bags supplied by the renowned company Kremer, based in Geneva. Some colors are extracted from precious substances like indigo and cochineal. There is the same Prussian blue that Turner used, a cobalt, an ultramarine blue, the luminous colors complemented by duller algae-like greens and golden, oxide-rich ochre tones. With the help of the artist's assistants, Toni and Jean-Philippe, the pigments are mixed with a vinyl medium and set out in buckets, a creamy paste that can be so thinned that it might become a spray of particles. The implements

FIG. 2

Untitled, 1977–78
Organic matter and glass | 39 $^3/_8$ x 31$^1/_2$ x 3 $^1/_2$ inches (100 x 80 x 8 cm)

FIG. 3

La suerte de matar, 1990 | Mixed media on canvas | 78 ³/₄ x 79 ⁷/₈ inches (200 x 203 cm)

Barceló uses to paint are largely adapted sculptors' tools, soft brushes like feather dusters that spread charcoal powder, paddles, a bayonet and wooden combs. Rather than depend on a roller, he prefers enormous brushes so that one gesture can span the entire width of his canvas.

Eight years ago he began watching cephalopods in aquariums, representing them as doubled, mirrored images. In the *Doble coleoidea* works on paper, their points of contact meet in the center of the sheet, whereas in the recent painting, *Doble CEPH.*, 2015, duplicated spheres read more like bulging eyes. When questioned about this lateral symmetry, he acknowledged being ambidextrous, "It's obvious: when I look at this work I see the

difference, but you cannot say which one is right. It's amusing because it is like a kind of portrait of the brain, left brain and right brain, also like things that reflect themselves in a mirror." [2]

The second group of paintings in this exhibition continues another theme, actually more a passion, which has also occupied the whole of his life. Barceló's initial images of bullfighting were posters commissioned for festivals; in 1988, he did one for Nîmes where the remains of the Roman amphitheater partly encircle the nineteenth-century arcades that shade the spectators facing the sun. In the paintings of 1990, the concave arena is seen from above, defined by a succession of rigid rings punctuated by dark recesses, at the bottom a sandy maelstrom. [FIG. 3] There are still similar overhead views, like *El ruedo*, 2016. "The first volcano I ever saw was Vesuvius in 1982, and I went down a little bit into its crater. Right away I had the impression that the crater was like a big empty bullfighting arena, enormous, as circular as the world, time and space. Something was about to happen, something dark, hot and dangerous was brewing. A perfect metaphor of life."[3] Lately the circular ribs might be flattened, and the paint applied in soft, overlapping waves narrowing to a ring. [FIG. 4]

The configuration was there in *Vésuvien*, 2013, and in a white bullfighting work, *Les arènes de Nîmes*, 2012 [FIG. 5]: "In this painting and surely in my life as well—there were centrifugal and centripetal forces working at the same time. Explosion and implosion."[4] Tellingly, the same force, the same psychological pressures, can transfer to a more abstract blue painting, what might be interpreted as a cosmic funnel in *Little Big Bang*, 2014.

FIG. 4

En redondo, April 2016 | Mixed media on canvas | 45 $^{1}/_{4}$ x 57 $^{1}/_{2}$ inches (115 x 146 cm)

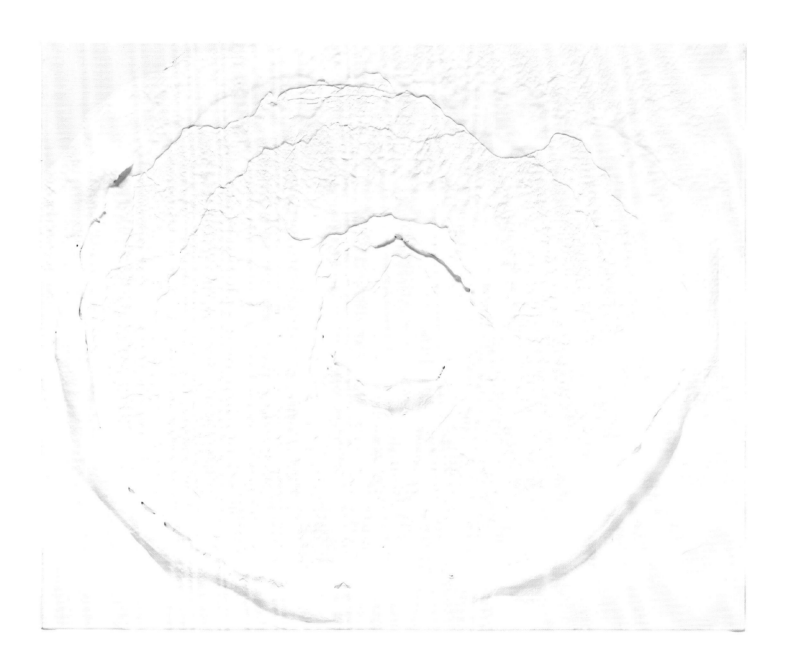

FIG. 4 | LEFT

En redondo [DETAIL], April 2016 | Mixed media on canvas | 45 $^1/_4$ x 57 $^1/_2$ inches (115 x 146 cm)

FIG. 5 | ABOVE

Les arènes de Nîmes, 2012 | Mixed media on linen | 32 $^1/_8$ x 39 $^3/_8$ inches (81.5 x 100 cm)

Private Collection

Many of the latest *corrida* paintings are different, less descriptive of the architecture, closer to an elegy. The radiant colors change within one painted arc from orange to rose, from saffron red to gold. The hairs on the brush or the abrasions of a metal comb or stylus leave raised lines, ridges not so different from those on a clay bowl made on a potter's wheel, but here the sweeping movement actively signifies tension, a crescendo of actions before an anticipated death.[5] From one new painting to the next, the focus is on ritual stages, the first bull of the afternoon, a solitary bullfighter who moves around the surface, as does the bull, until suddenly he is almost hidden, clinging to the side of the stretcher, or in *Cite*, 2016, the juxtaposition is lateral, like two hand grips, bull on left, a standing man on the right, outlined in ghostly white. [FIG. 6] In another painting, *Esquinero*, 2016, minute touches, almost an accidental stain, correspond to the dark bull merging with the toreador's gold and magenta cape flying off the right side.

FIG. 6 | ABOVE
Cite, June 2016 | Mixed media on canvas | 46 ^{1}/$_2$ x 82 ^{5}/$_8$ inches (118 x 210 cm)

FIG. 6 | RIGHT
Cite [DETAIL]

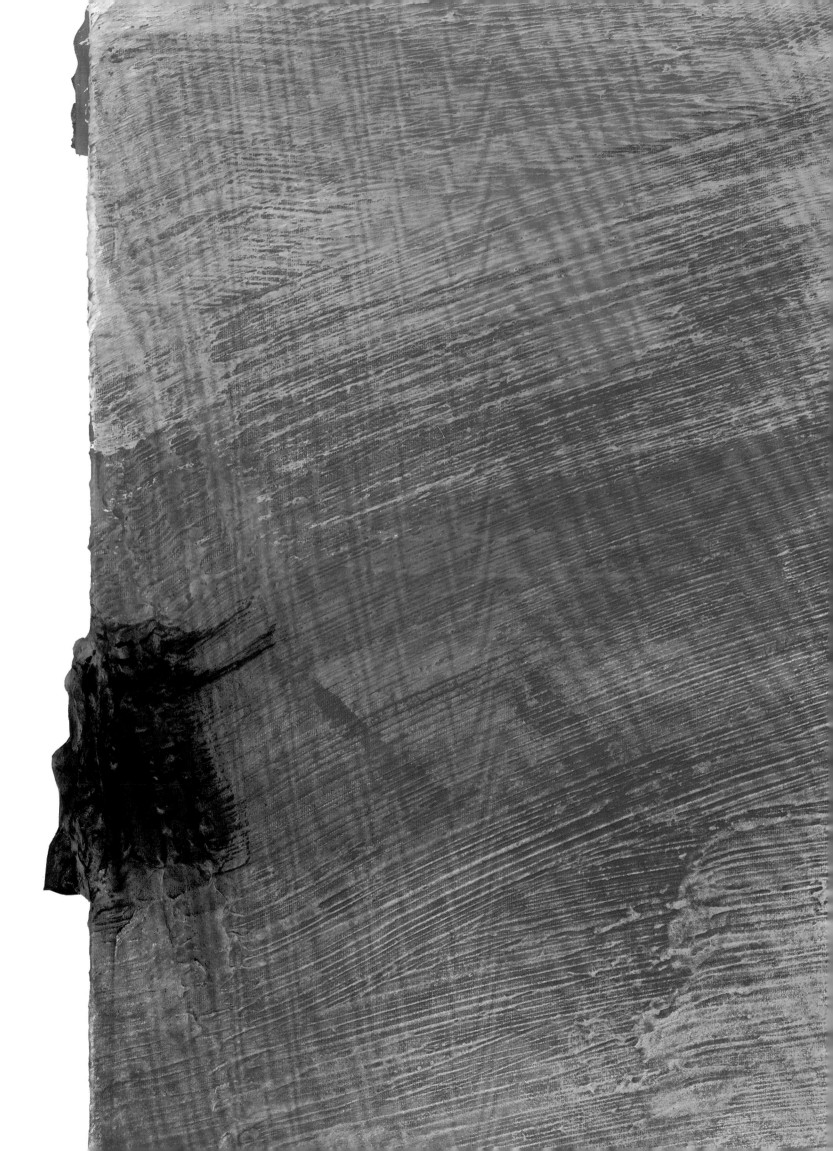

FIG. 7 | ABOVE
Paseillo avec taureau, 2015 | Engraving, aquatint, etching and drypoint | 22 x 30^{1}/8 inches (56 x 76.5 cm)

FIG. 8 | OPPOSITE
Miquel Barceló and **Josef Nadj** | *Paso doble* | Bandiagara Escarpment, Dogon country of Mali, 2009

Like their breeders, Barceló recognizes which animals have the *cara*, or courage, to enter the ring; and he follows contemporary heroes in the sport, particularly José Tomás and his extraordinary, quiet way of moving and addressing the bull. The graphic works which have occupied much of Barceló's time in the last two years are more narrative, for example, the opening ceremony, the *paseillo*, is depicted in a 2015 image; a giant bull gazes down on the men and horses in the arena, his pale horns spread as if to encompass, almost bless, the crowd.[6] [FIG. 7] In another work, a flurry of black lines indicates the harpoon-pointed sticks that are thrust into the animal, the *banderillas*.

Barceló is aware that bullfighting is appreciated by a dwindling audience but the politics are not his concern, nor is his affinity to the sport something bound by nostalgia or folklore. He responds to the aesthetic, and explains that at the beginning of the twentieth century the toreadors changed their way of approaching the bull and began walking in a circular motion while the bull moved from side to side; the choreography became more like modern dance where a single figure is often isolated. "After each bull they clean the arena, the sand, the blood, just like you wipe clean a blackboard after a lesson in order to begin again," and for this reason the action connects to the most daring gestural movements, and the sound of the painter's brush, his secret, unrepeatable life, "that which remains is the thing that has happened, the pleasure is in the past."[7]

A PERIPHERAL KINGDOM

One of the great losses in Barceló's life has been his freedom to settle in Mali for part of every year as he did annually from 1988 to 2008.[8] In tribute to his African community, Barceló staged *Paso doble* in the Dogon country for November 2009. He explained what happened to Éric Mézil (who was working for the Festival in Avignon when the two-person performance featuring Barceló and the choreographer, Josef Nadj, premiered there in summer 2006). Under the overhanging rocks of Bandiagara, a thick clay floor and angled wall were constructed and a supply of still damp earthenware jars readied, these *aufàbies* as they are called in Spain, resembled those that in this remote region hold fermented millet beer. As *Paso doble* progresses, the protagonists are armed with the pots and the action becomes violent. Barceló seemed to be the sole survivor on this night until Nadj suddenly moved and the audience, the entire village, applauded. "At the moment when I planted the *banderillas* in the clay, in the pots that were on Nadj's head, people really cried and thought that I had killed him. They thought that it was a sacrifice, something which is actually very familiar to them from their culture and history. As well as that, they know clay better than most people, they know what it is, they know how heavy it is and that it restricts breathing. They were worried for Nadj who was under this pile of clay. So they applauded when they saw a sort of resurrection! A reincarnation of his spirit like in Chauvet's parietal art!"[9] [FIG. 8]

Parietal, as the dictionary defines it, is a word that relates to the wall of the body, or its cavity, and in archaeology it refers to prehistoric art found on rock walls. This explains why this odd term is frequently applied to Barceló, reinforced by his twenty-year association with the caves at Chauvet in southern France. Only rediscovered in 1994, these deep chambers lie under the natural stone Pont d'Arc which spans the Ardèche river valley. The only people allowed in are a limited number of scientists, conservationists, and a few invited guests. Barceló is on the scientific committee and during his last visit to Chauvet, accompanied by the chief custodian, Marie Bardisa, he knelt down on one walkway, and from there had his first view of a large lion, its contour circumscribing the heads of three lions also facing right. [FIG. 9]

In these caves, the hand of individuals can be identified, particularly the artist with a broken finger, and the images of the horses, bison, bears, along with "indeterminate" beasts, are surprisingly varied. Unlike in caves of a later date (here the art is more than 30,000 years old), there is a clear empathy between man and animal. The techniques also differ and anticipate classic methods. A stump was devised to smudge the crushed pigment applied to the clay surface and to deliberately create a sense of volume and shadow. There are grids made of red ochre dots stamped onto the ground, perhaps with a fiber pad, and in places, using a human hand as a stencil, a spray of powdered ochre surrounds the unmistakable form. [FIG. 10]

FIG. 9 | LEFT

The artist in the cave at Chauvet

FIG. 10 | ABOVE

Cave painting from Chauvet

Barceló's ease in fitting into different cultures and epochs, his ambitious public art works (the ceiling at the United Nations in Geneva, the chapel in the Cathedral in Palma), the many shows in ceramics museums, the display on the walls of the grand Palais des Papes in Avignon and most recently a great wall made of modelled faces/hole-pierced bricks situated in the crypt of the Musée Picasso, are these ventures and prestigious locations a hindrance to the recognition of Barceló's achievement as a contemporary painter? Where does he belong? There are portraits and self-portraits from every period and an infinite number of illustrated diaries and sketchbooks. There are recurring series of "abstract" studies of waves and grottos. He first appeared on the international stage alongside artists like David Salle and Jean-Michel Basquiat in the 1982 Kassel Documenta 7 and exhibited at the Leo Castelli Gallery in 1987. The curator of Documenta, Rudi Fuchs, made an acute observation. When he first went to the studio he responded to the velocity and formal freedom of this previously unknown artist, "What at some point was considered frivolous or just caprice, Miró's swiftness, Barceló was able to exploit as a way out of the formal slowness of the older generation in Spain."[10] Fuchs and others could see Barceló was moving away from the defining post-war figures like Antoni Tàpies, Antonio Saura and Eduardo Chillida, their economy, their tendency to eschew color; instead Barceló's bravura and his lively record of organic and human life measured up to the imaginative output of recently established artists like Francesco Clemente and René Daniels. Meanwhile, Barceló resisted being defined as a Spanish artist, not least for any association with the Spain of *franquismo*. After the 1980s, the trail of mixed exhibitions almost dries up. Enrique Juncosa and I curated a solo show at the Whitechapel Gallery in London and at IVAM Valencia in 1994–95, and the amazing results of Barceló's engagement with Africa formed a presentation in Dublin in 2008, however, Barceló's work has hardly been shown or collected in museums in Anglo-Saxon countries, and strangely this artist who finds himself more and more in Asia, is hardly to be found in international biennales.

When the simultaneous exhibitions at the Musée Picasso and at the Bibliothèque Nationale de France opened in Paris in March 2016, interviewers asked for Barceló's reaction to being compared to Picasso, both men so prodigious in every branch of art, both arriving in Paris after first getting noticed in Barcelona. Barceló responded that his galaxy of painter-heroes goes back to Rembrandt and Tintoretto and extends to many unnamed artists. He is the proud owner of a 1909 Picasso drawing of a small pitcher [FIG. 11], and also a 1914 collage of a glass where sand is applied to demarcate shade. Ignoring the presumption of being the heir to Picasso, the artist referred to their shared culture, adding a novel idea to cubist theory, reminding us of the central tenet of Hispanic Catholicism, that of the Trinity, that one is really three. Taken as a metaphysical idea, Picasso's decision to represent multiple points of view within a single image had a precedent.

In the spring of 2016 one of Barceló's obsessions has been to prepare parchment derived from goat skin, the kind associated with legal documents, as the ground for tender, amusing portraits of his mother posing at the age of ninety. A painter herself, she kept a collection of art books, amongst them the slim monographs in the Argentinean series, *Pinacoteca de los genios*, and Barceló came to respect little-known artists.[11] One was Pedro Figari (1861–1938) whose painted views of Montevideo are rendered in a style somewhat like Bonnard's, his subjects extending to black women and brothels.[12] "I really like literature and stories about painters. I read the lives of painters the way they used to read the lives of the saints... I feed on them." Time and again, Barceló returns to the achievements of related disciplines in Mallorca. In the thirteenth and fourteenth centuries, there were skilled people making glass, and those using the local mud for bricks and pots, as well as those trained to build houses and churches. The remarkable architect, Guillem Sagrera (c.1380–1456), another native of Felanitx, was bidden to the court at Naples to work on the Castel Nuovo; one looks

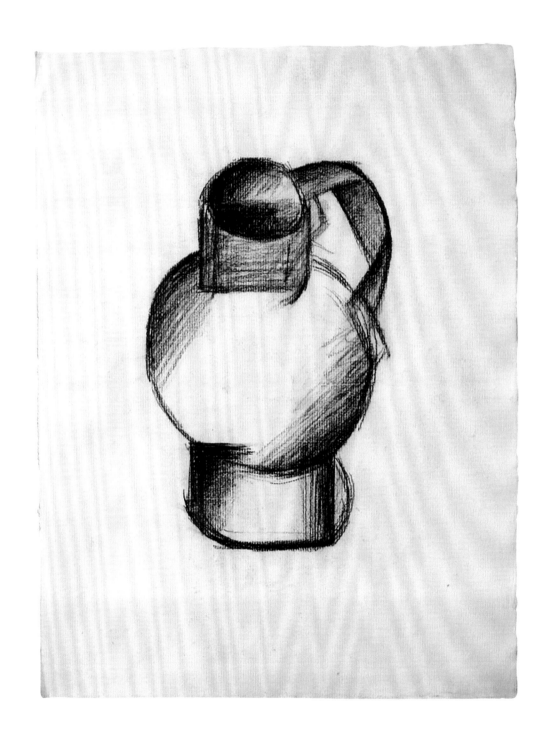

FIG. 11

Pablo Picasso | *Le pichet*, Autumn 1909

Charcoal on paper | 12 $^3/_8$ x 9 $^7/_8$ inches (31.4 x 25.1 cm)

Collection of Miquel Barceló

FIG. 12

Detail of vault by architect Guillem Sagrera, 1452 | Room of Barons, Castel Nuovo, Naples

at his glorious vault there, a star with eight points, and thinks of a starfish or flower as well as a motif from Islamic art. [FIG. 12] Mallorca also had a famous cartography school, notably the work of the Cresques family whose map of the Mediterranean, made c.1375, now in the Bibliothèque Nationale, extended the familiar territory to register the distant Niger River, a feature that had to be re-introduced centuries later when Africa was explored by Europeans.[13]

Like many artists, Barceló's education was extended when he began to travel, going to Italy in 1974 to see early Renaissance art, and there discovering modernists like Carlo Scarpa and Lucio Fontana. Jackson Pollock, Joseph Beuys and Cy Twombly were inspirational figures, and along with other young Catalans, he responded to Guy Debord and the Situationists.[14] But when we try to compare those artists who emerged in the 1970s and '80s, the discussion gets complicated as their paths are so individual and the whole idea of a school or a defense of painting anathema.[15] The common ground surfaces more often through literature and language. Gaston Bachelard's essays, for example, *The Poetics of Space*, resonate with this generation, and Miquel continues to read him (and lately Montaigne). I open one of Bachelard's books in translation and turn to the essay, *Dynamic and Material Imagination*; it introduces "isomorphic images," those interwoven by "oneiric communion." Bachelard, who regularly brings in other writers, sounds as if he's describing Barceló's art:

> Here flowing hair will know the night of caves that
> lie beneath the sea, just as the sea knows the plant's
> subterranean dreams. The dark night of the depths
> summons all these images not to the firmament's vast,
> dark unity, but rather to that matter made of darkness
> itself, which is the earth, earth which the very roots
> digest. Whether we digest or bury in the earth, we follow
> the path of the very same transcendence; here, Jean
> Wahl is our guide, though we are probably interpreting his
> words more materially than he would wish:

> *In the depths where a man can be so very comfortable,*
> *In the primal clay of the flesh...*
> *I am plunged deep...*
> *In the unknown land, where my unknowing brings the dawn?*[16]

Particularly wild, unleashed and hybrid images populate Barceló's drawings, suggesting a kind of delirium, an exorcism. The artist cautions that you fear what you want. One thinks of his *Les 120 Journées, Pornográfica*, Lanzarote published in 2000 [FIG. 13], and the illustrations to Dante's *Commedia* that followed in 2003, a volume each for hell, purgatory and paradise. Barceló takes particular pride and inspiration from one forebear, Ramon Llull (c. 1233–1315), the great Mallorcan writer who began his adult life as courtier and libertine. Harold Bloom, the American literary scholar, relates how Llull became an amazing autodidact, devouring the Bible, Talmud, Koran, Plato, Aristotle and vast quantities of medicinal and natural history. A brilliant linguist, he absorbed Arabic and Hebrew, and with his *Art of Arts*, "Ramon then began his scandalous literary productivity, writing more copiously than any scholar can hope to read him."[17] Bloom's reaction goes further,

> By this I mean erotic intensity, which brings up the oddity
> of so ecstatic a work, since both the Lover, Blanquerna,
> and God are males. Sufi analogues abound, but I hardly
> see how homoerotic overtones are to be evaded in this
> Christian Platonic rhapsody which employs Court of Love
> Troubadour themes. Llull's God is hardly a beautiful Arab
> boy, and yet the Sufi overtones are always there. Fusion or
> union with the Beloved is not part of Llull's figuration; we
> are a long way from the Spiritual Canticle [of St. John of
> the Cross]. And yet we are left with the pathos of Ramon
> Llull, Catalan-of-Catalans, Mallorcan-of-Mallorcans. His
> final sense of defeat is eloquent in his song of Ramon:

> *I have taken on too great a task.*
> *I have sought a vast project in this world...*
> *I want to die on the high seas of love.*[18]

P.A $\frac{5}{5}$

FIG. 13
Les 120 Journées, série Pornográfica, Lanzarote, 2000 │ Etching and aquatint │ 29 $^1/_2$ x 36 $^1/_4$ inches (75 x 92 cm)

FIG. 14

Untitled, 2016 | Ceramic | 21 $^5/_8$ x 21 $^1/_4$ x 4 $^3/_8$ inches (55 x 54 x 11 cm)

IMAGES "MUCH OLDER THAN ONE COULD IMAGINE"

Barceló regards terracotta as the mother of art and he has referenced so many things in clay—meteors, deserts, octopus, grapes, and frequently his own head.[19] He begins with an abundant stock of vessels, and rapidly manipulates the damp clay surfaces, using every possible kind of touch, elbow as well as finger and bone. The soft walls are twisted, cut, violently ruptured, caressed, and sometimes colored with unusual formulas for the glazes. The swelling parts, and hollow forms, the topography is enhanced by pathways identified with soot-like deposits. When a work has been fired, the human activity leaves a particular trace. Barceló can stare at an almost immaculate surface and identify the vestige of his finger, shirt sleeve, his touch.

"Doubt is that type of anxiety, or anguish, about sinking into melancholy. You never master that. You work more often with suspicions and intuitions, just like with intuitions about materials that often prove to be right and are sometimes failures. But failures are magnificent, there is nothing, but why not, it has its place...."[20]

Lately, Barceló has been re-imagining an upright female body lying down, the vessel now a platter, rendered in the white, almost porcelain-like clay of Mallorca. [FIG. 14] The swelling breasts and stomach, her crevices, the triangular shape associated with the depiction of the female vulva in ancient cultures, the sense of intimacy and specificity is extreme for this artist. Could you claim that these works relate to the spores and phallic protrusions in the blue paintings? The artist wrote recently, "The end of the nose, the tips of the fingers, genitals and breast...These are the soft parts that are before our eyes and at the forefront of our thoughts. They are fragile but they are what controls the darkness in front of us."[21] All his work projects reverence, anguish, horror, vulnerability, an art that evolves as strangely seductive and curiously medieval.

When Barceló's visitors are taken to the former brick factory at Vilafranca de Bonany (which now belongs to the artist), they are shown the *teulera*, what he calls a "crocodile pond," a pit where failed pots are thrown and gradually rehydrated. Nearby, a floor to ceiling wall was replaced with glass which was washed with thinned-down clay. Barceló filled it with drawings, smearing away portions with his fingers so the strong outdoor light casts ever-changing shadows on the floor. This idea was inspired by the whitewashed windows with daily menus in the Paris suburb of Meudon (where he has had a working space) and the natural temptation to draw on any surface covered with condensation. He adapted the technique this year to create a huge 196-meter fresco in the Bibliothèque Nationale, again using thinned clay from Mallorca, the panels of glass filled with a succession of skeletons, fish, animals and vegetables. [FIG. 15] The result was mesmerizing, a kind of contemporary parietal art, complete with fertility images as well as a beautiful sense of decoration and movement, the patterns like those on the light-penetrated floor of the sea or forest. [FIG. 16] Llull too had a strong feeling for nature, as Gerald Brenan reminds us, "the sight of trees and stars and moonlight moved him to contemplations – and his general disposition was eager and optimistic."[22]

FIG. 15 | OPPOSITE
Le Grand Verre de terre - Vidre de meravelles, [DETAIL], 2016 | Scratched clay on windows of the Julien-Cain aisle of the François Miterrand site – Bibliothèque nationale de France, on view March 22 - August 28, 2016

FIG. 16 | NEXT SPREAD
Le Grand Verre de terre - Vidre de meravelles, 2016 | Scratched clay on windows of the Julien-Cain aisle of the François Miterrand site – Bibliothèque nationale de France, on view March 22 - August 28, 2016

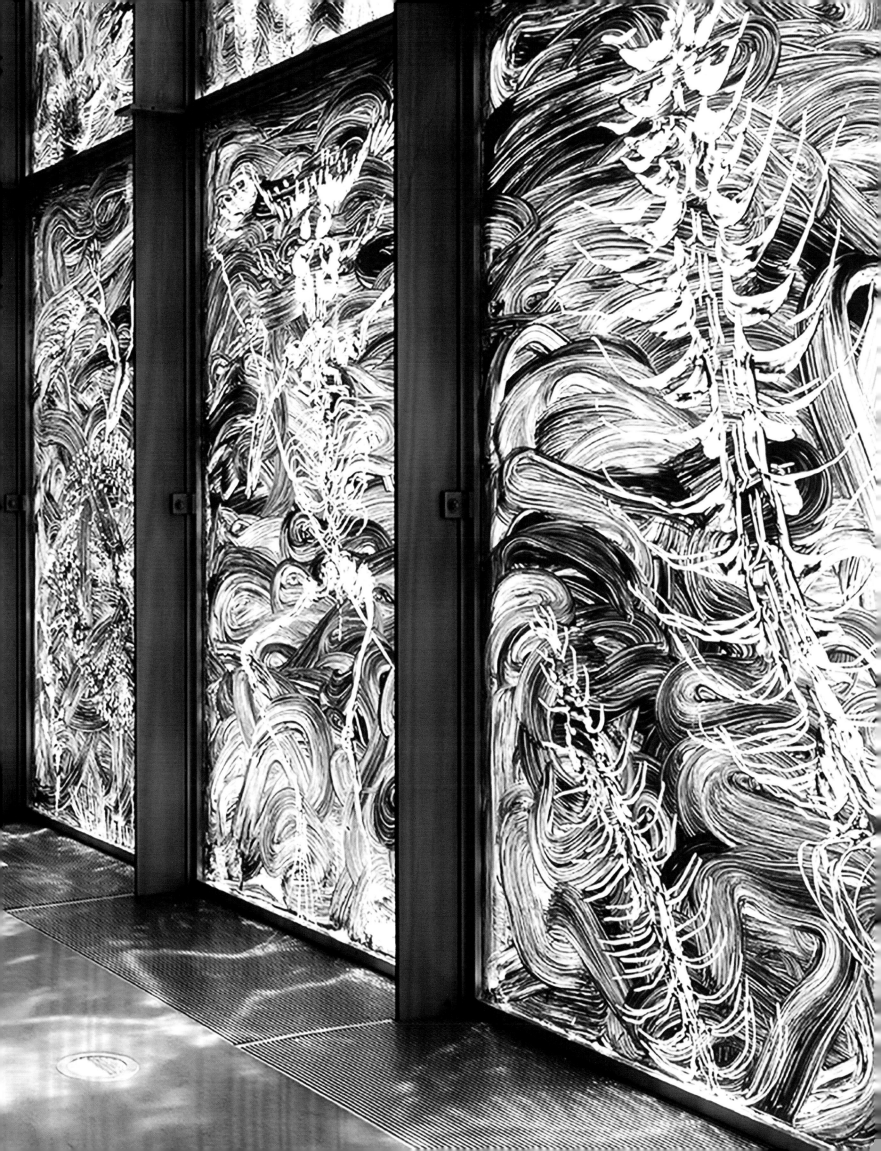

When I'm shown around the studio, the work in progress also reminds me of what is said about the late eighteenth-century poets and scientists, those who depended upon speculation and intuition as well as empirical data, those who devised original instruments and were talented in many spheres. For example, William Herschel taught music as his livelihood and meanwhile invented and cast the special mirrors for his large telescopes. With the help of his faithful, talented sister, Caroline, he spent months scanning the night sky before their unexpected discovery of Uranus in 1781. In his fascinating book, *The Age of Wonder*, Richard Holmes quotes a famous sonnet by John Keats comparing Herschel's recognition of the new planet with George Chapman's Elizabethan translation of Homer, "Then felt I like some watcher of the skies / When a new planet swims into his ken."[23] This is how I interpret Miquel's mind imaginatively sailing through the ocean of stars and vicariously entering the strangely serene action in the bullring, buffeted by wave after wave, his liquid paint curling, flowing and acting of its own accord, his lament for friends like the poet Hervé Guilbert. As he gets older we come to believe his disavowal of a fixed identity, "Je suis d'outre-mer, je ne suis pas d'ici"; despite saying this, he did admit that his roots are in Western painting, especially the pictures on the walls of the Prado. He identifies with the carnal nature of a fellow Spaniard like Goya, another life-long companion.[24]

NOTE: Unless otherwise noted, all quotes from the artist were in conversation with Catherine Lampert, May 2016.

1
Interview in the catalogue *Barceló before Barceló, 1973-1982*, published by Galaxia Gutenberg, Círculo de Lectores, Barcelona, 2009, p. 306. The accompanying exhibition began at the Fundación Pilar i Joan Miró, Palma, Mallorca.

2
"Interview with Eric Mézil," *Miquel Barceló: Terramare*, Palais des Papes, Petit Palais, Collection Lambert, Avignon, 2010, p. 233.

3
The artist, *Miquel Barceló: Courant Central*, Ben Brown Fine Arts, Hong Kong, 2014, p. 28.

4
Ibid, p. 16.

5
He reminds us that the tradition of bullfighting also links to a region somewhere beyond concentrations of people, indeed the farms in the center of Spain where the bulls are raised must be exceptionally large. The breed isn't suitable for meat, the animals are fed acorns from the cork trees. Before entering the ring, they are not allowed to see men except on horseback. At the age of two, they are tested for their aggression and strength, their intelligence, judged by the muscles over the shoulder and neck that give the distinctive profile of the *toro bravo*.

6
When he began to address the subject of bullfighting more than twenty-five years ago, Barceló was aware that in art this very Spanish subject veered dangerously close to folklore, ("La tauromachie, pour moi, c'est un peu dérisoire"), *Sol y Sombra. Miquel Barceló*, co-published by Actes Sud, La Bibliothèque nationale de France and Musée national Picasso-Paris, Paris, 2016, p. 124. He adds to this qualification that his recent bullfighting works are not conceived in an ironic spirit, nor a nostalgic one. Naturally the artist is aware how political the subject has become, not least in Catalonia, and how much resistance there is to the continuation of all "blood" sports. Where he lives in Mallorca is a farm with pigs, goats and sheep. His studio was once a stable, the property, a former hunting lodge, adjoining a tower that is 1000 years old, and behind it a steep mountain. Late in the autumn, the *fer matances* is celebrated, a pig is slaughtered, friends gather and the beginning of winter is marked by the eating of the first *sobrasada*, the event a continuation of an ancient ritual. See Amélie Aranguren, "La matanza del cerdo y otras conjeturas sobre vasijas," *Miquel Barceló. Conjeturas sobre vasijas*, "la Caixa" Banca Privada/Factum Arte, Barcelona, 2008.

7
Interview with Émilia Philippot, *Sol y Sombra*, 2016, p. 124. "Après chaque taureau, on nettoie l'arène, le sable, le sang, comme on efface un tableau noir d'école après une leçon pour recommencer. Tu vois toutes les traces des taureaux, tous leurs mouvements: ce sont souvent des mouvements circulaires," and for this reason the arena connects to painting, "c'est ce qui reste de quelque chose de passé: le plaisir est passé."

8
He was advised by intelligence agencies that he was a potential target for extremists.

9
Terramare, 2010, pp. 240 - 41. A film directed by Isaki Lacuesta, *El cuaderno de barro*, 2012, documents this event.

10
Rudi Fuchs, *Barceló before Barceló*, 2009, p. 260.

11
"Vivarium, Francisca Artigues," an exhibition of his mother's embroidered images, based on Miquel's drawings, was shown at the Textilmuseum St. Gallen in 2015.

12
Terramare, 2010, p. 239.

13
Ibid, p. 227. "In Majorca there was a very great cartography school where they drew the first map of the world with Africa and the Niger River represented. Immense - that's all you can see on this map of the world! There are things that we knew at that time that we forgot straight away. We had to wait until Rene Caillié arrived in Timbuktu, to realise that we had forgotten the existence of the Niger River. It's a magnificent story. There was a famous family of cartographers in Majorca, Jafuda Cresques and his children. It was a great family who founded a school - one of the maps is in the Bibliothèque Nationale de France in Paris."

14
Barceló before Barceló, 2009, p. 260.

15
For example, Peter Schjeldahl reviewing Albert Oehlen's exhibition in the New Museum in the New York began, "German artist Albert Oehlen is the foremost painter of the era that has seen painting decline as the chief medium of new art. It's a dethronement that he honestly registers and oddly celebrates, as can be seen in *Home and Garden*," *New Yorker*, June 22, 2015.

16
Mary McAllester Jones, *Gaston Bachelard, Subversive Humanist*, Madison, Wisconsin, 1991, pp. 108-9.

17
Harold Bloom, Ramon Llull and Catalan Tradition, Institut Ramon Llull, Barcelona, 2006, p. 33.

18
Ibid, pp. 33-35.

19
See *Miquel Barceló. Conjeturas sobre vasijas*, Barcelona, 2008, with images from the Museo de Cerámica of Barcelona.

20
Terramare, 2010, p. 239.

21
Miquel Barceló: Courant Central, 2014, p. 60.

22
Gerald Brenan, *The Literature of the Spanish People*, New York, 1957, p. 106.

23
Richard Holmes, *The Age of Wonder, How the Romantic Generation Discovered the Beauty and Terror of Science*, London, 2009, p. 113. The quote is from John Keats, *On First Looking into Chapman's Homer*, 1816.

24
Sol y Sombra, 2016, p. 126

PLATE 1

Little Big Bang, 2014
Mixed media on canvas
$23^5/8$ x $31^1/2$ inches (60 x 80 cm)

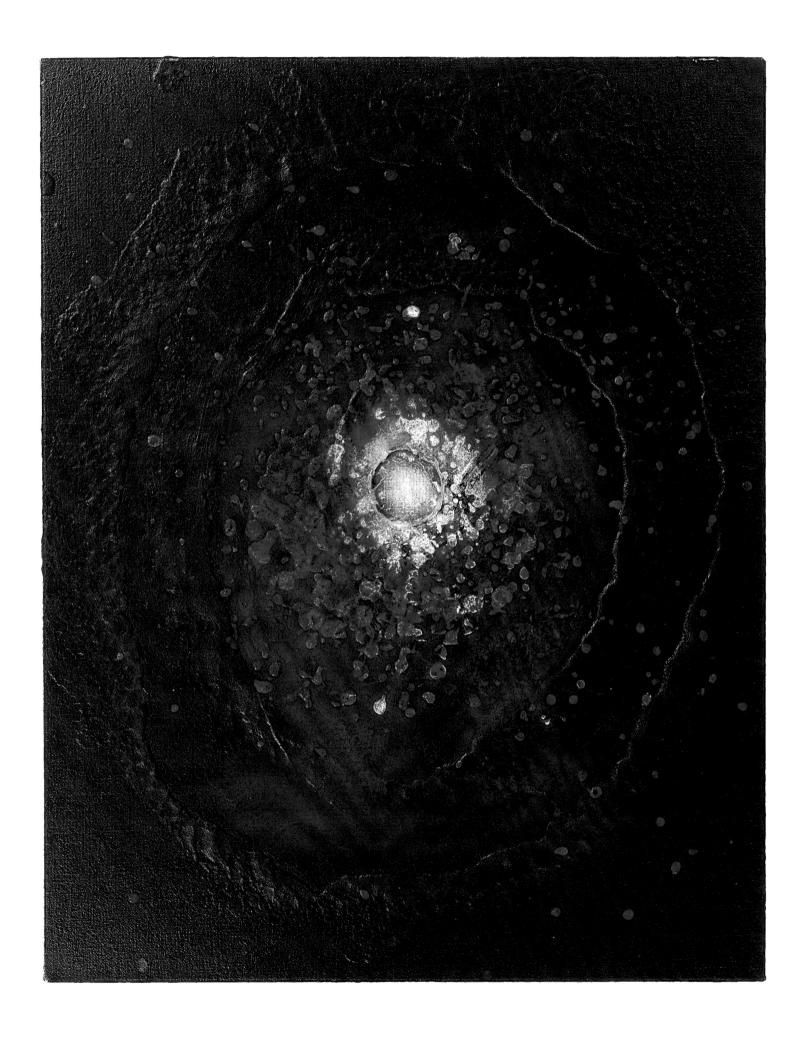

PLATE 2

Petit cosmos, 2015
Mixed media on canvas
39 3/8 x 31 7/8 inches (100 x 81 cm)

Pop blau, 2015
Mixed media on canvas
32 $^{1}/_{4}$ x 36 $^{5}/_{8}$ inches (82 x 93 cm)

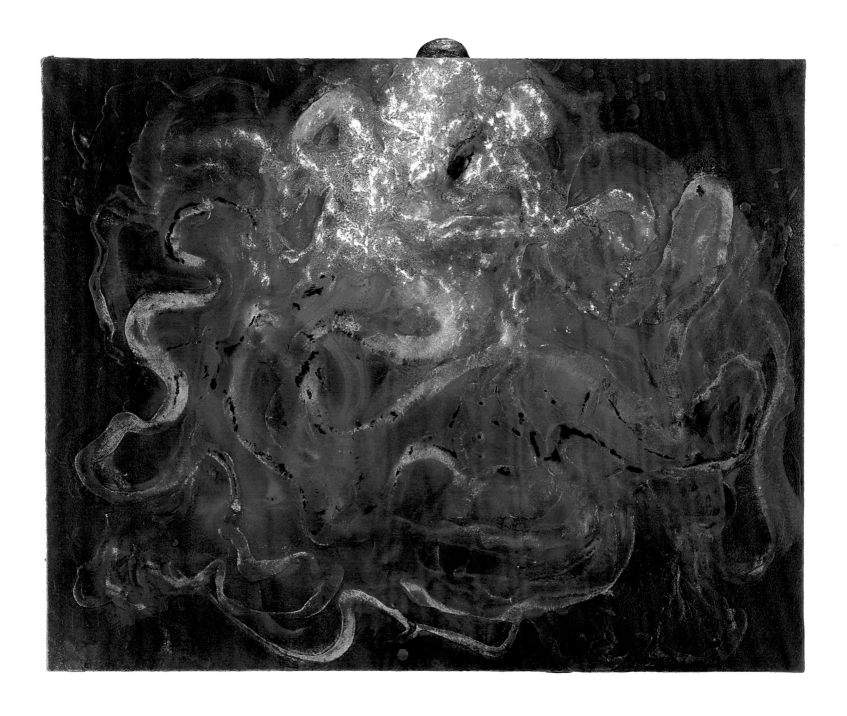

Pop de fonera, 2015
Mixed media on canvas
$33\frac{1}{2}$ x $41\frac{3}{8}$ inches (85 x 105 cm)

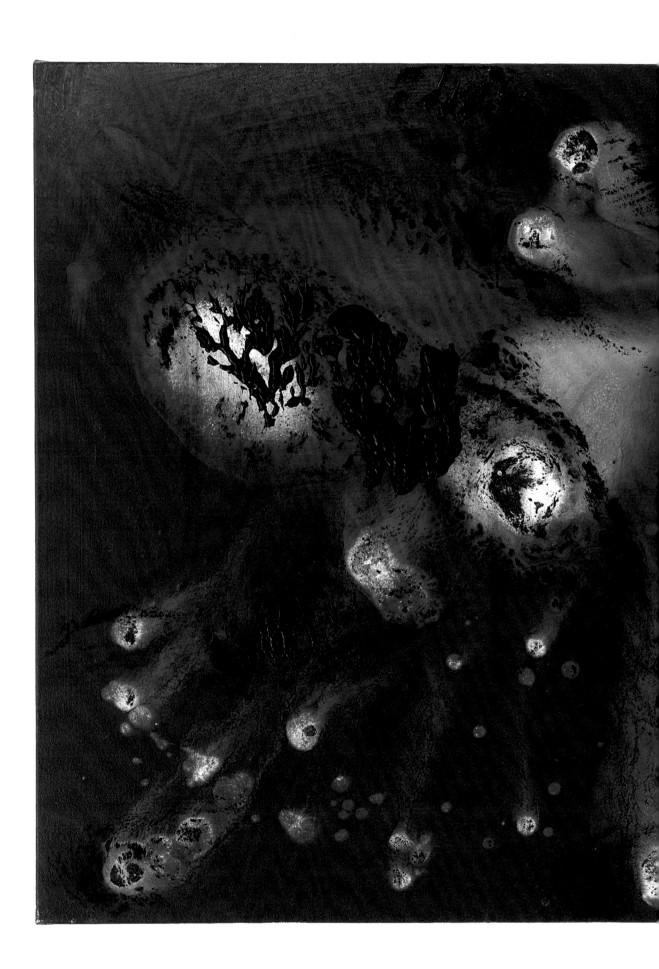

PLATE 5

Doble CEPH., 2015 | Mixed media on canvas | 48 $^7/_8$ x 77 $^3/_4$ inches (114 x 195 cm)

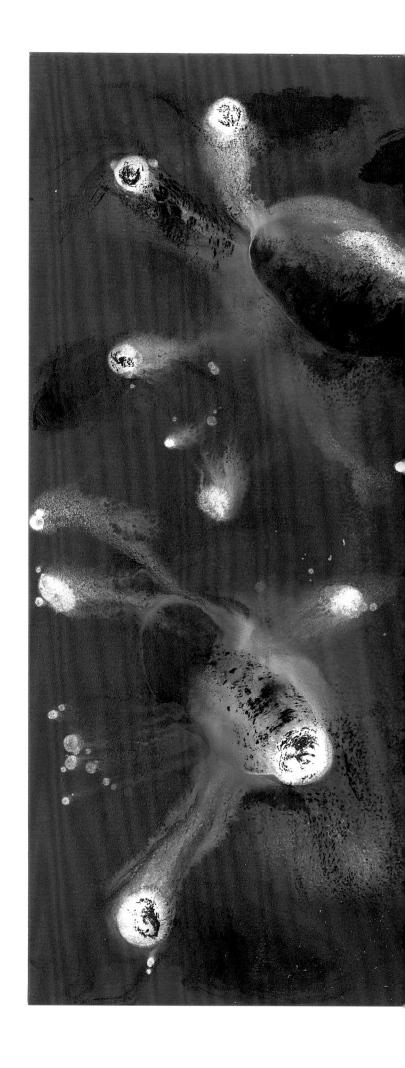

Larvaire, 2015
Mixed media on canvas
74 ^{7}/$_8$ x 94 ^{1}/$_2$ inches (190 x 240 cm)

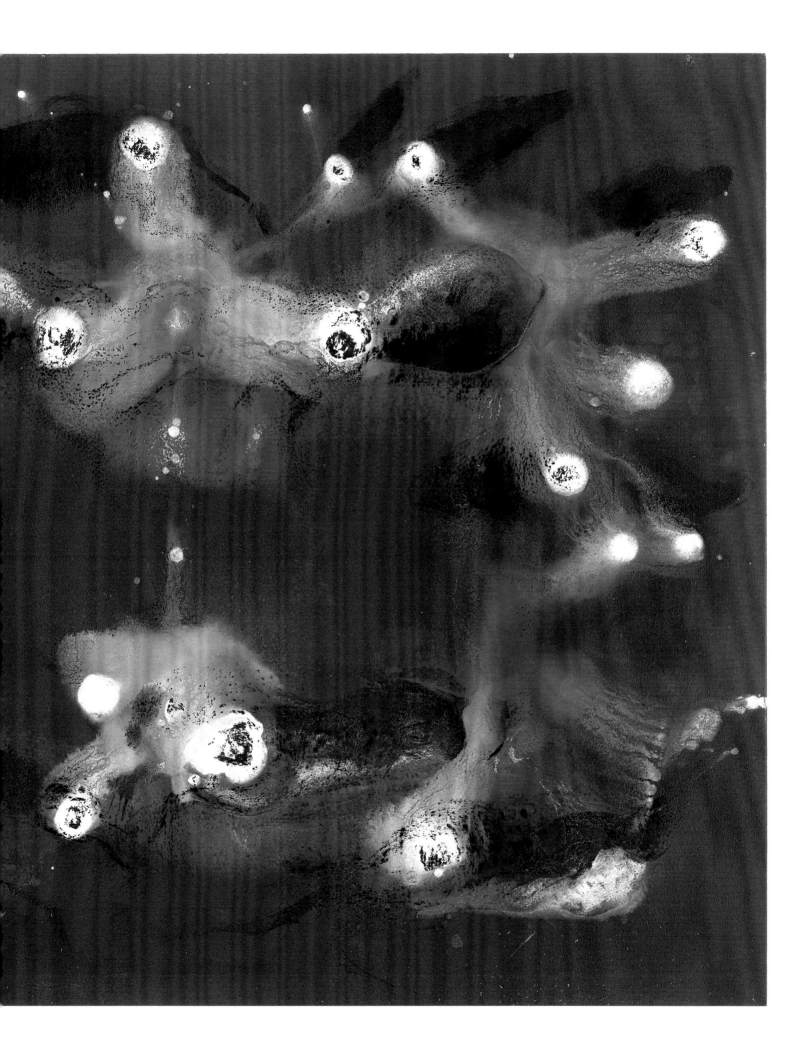

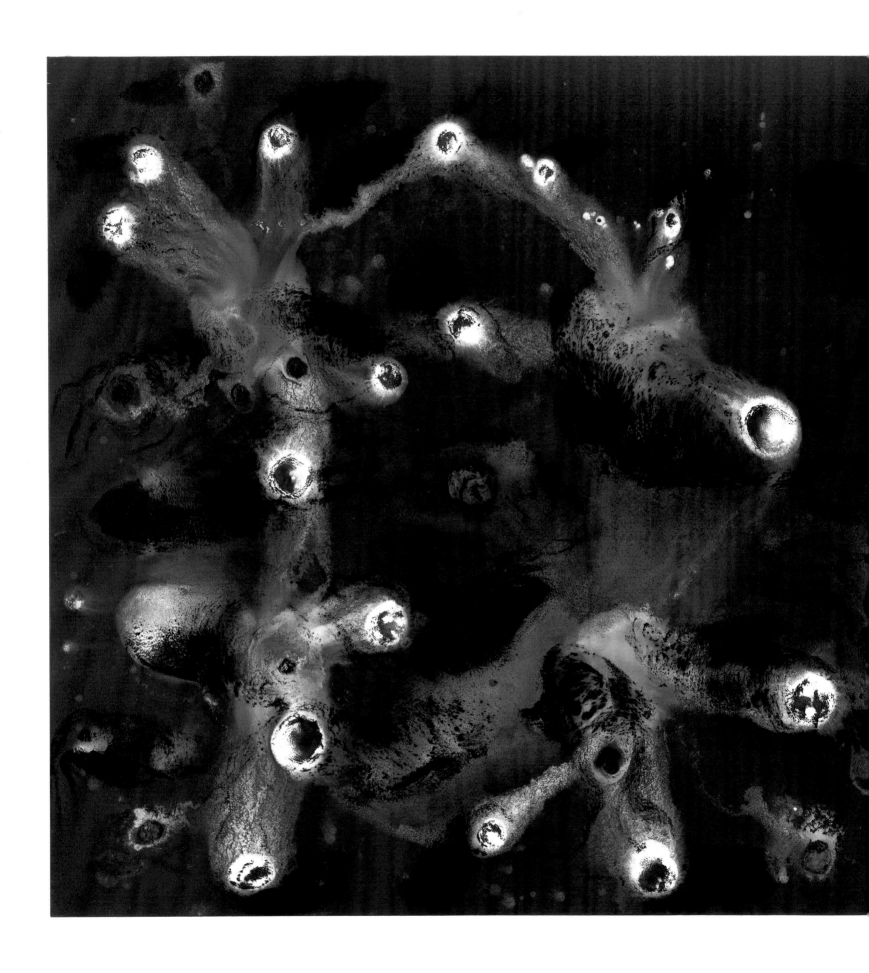

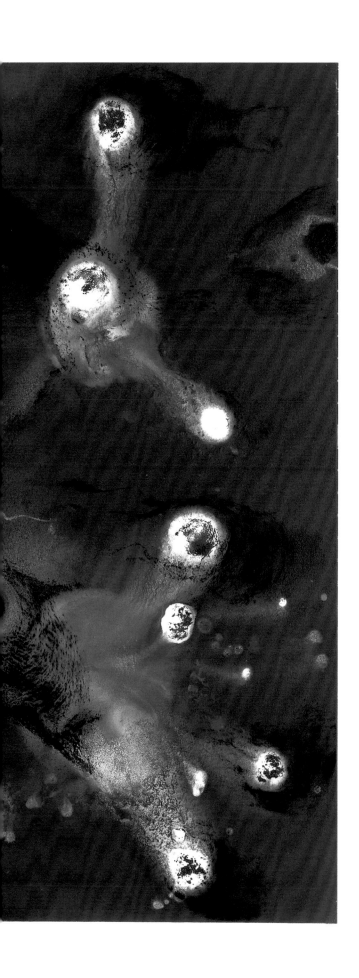

PLATE 7
De·Profundis, 2015
Mixed media on canvas
74 ^{3}/4 x 106 ^{1}/4 inches (190 x 270 cm)

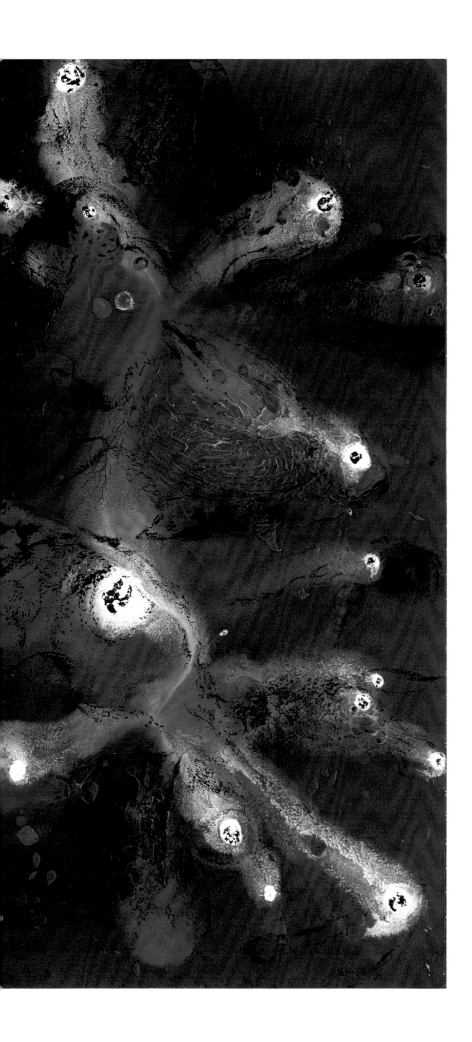

PLATE 8

Kraken central, 2015
Mixed media on canvas
74 $^3/_4$ x 106 $^1/_4$ inches (190 x 270 cm)

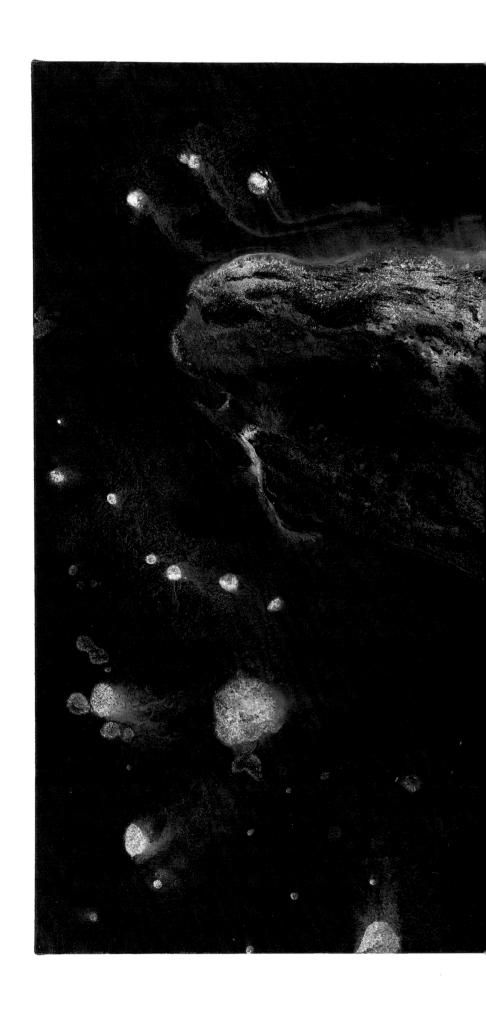

PLATE 9
Sipiota, 2015
Mixed media on canvas
51 $^1/_8$ x 77 $^3/_4$ inches (130 x 195 cm)

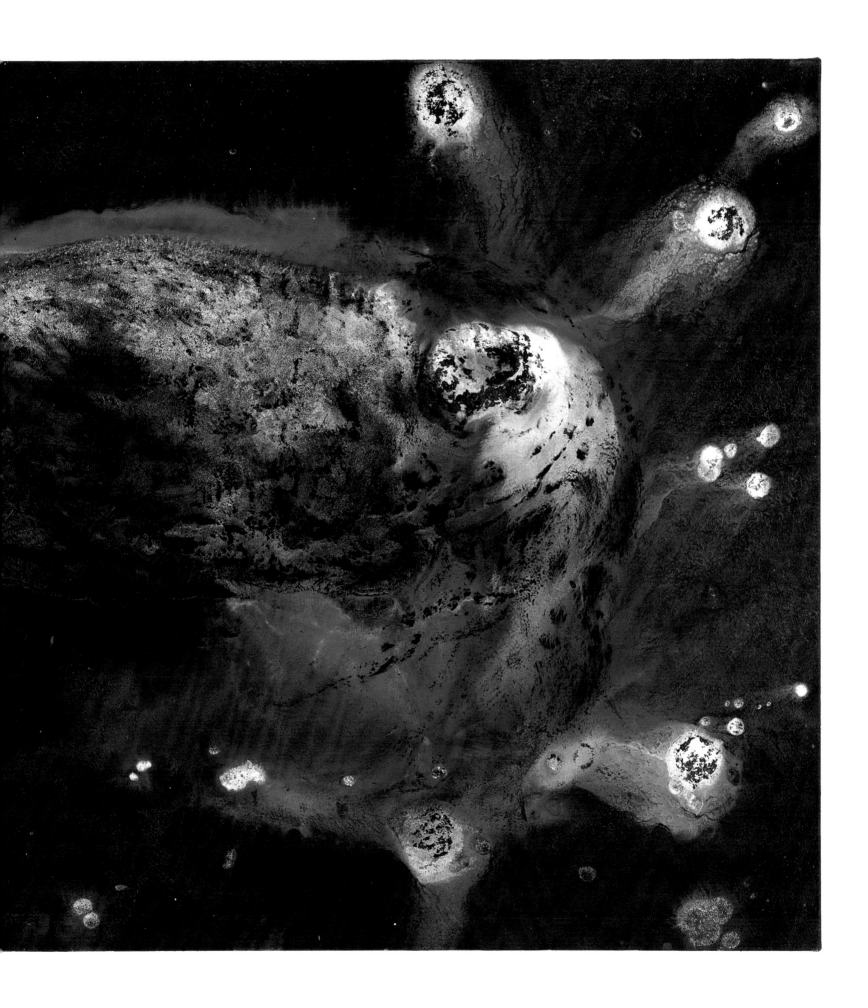

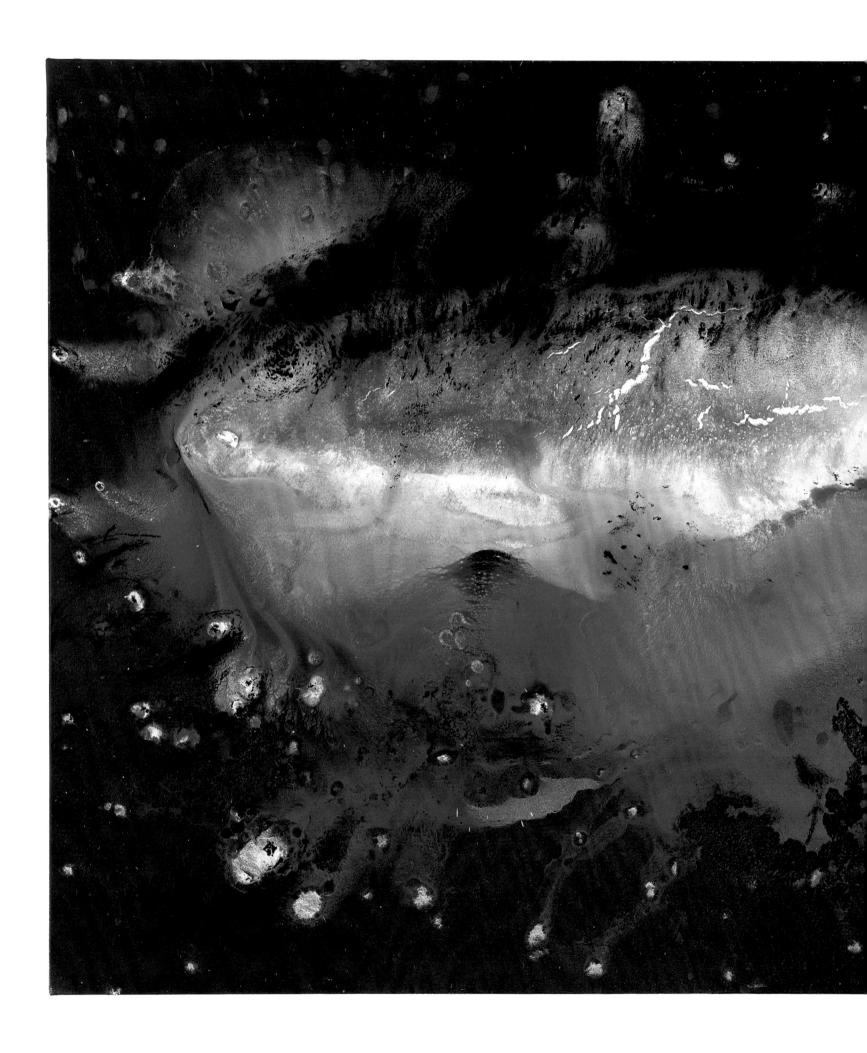

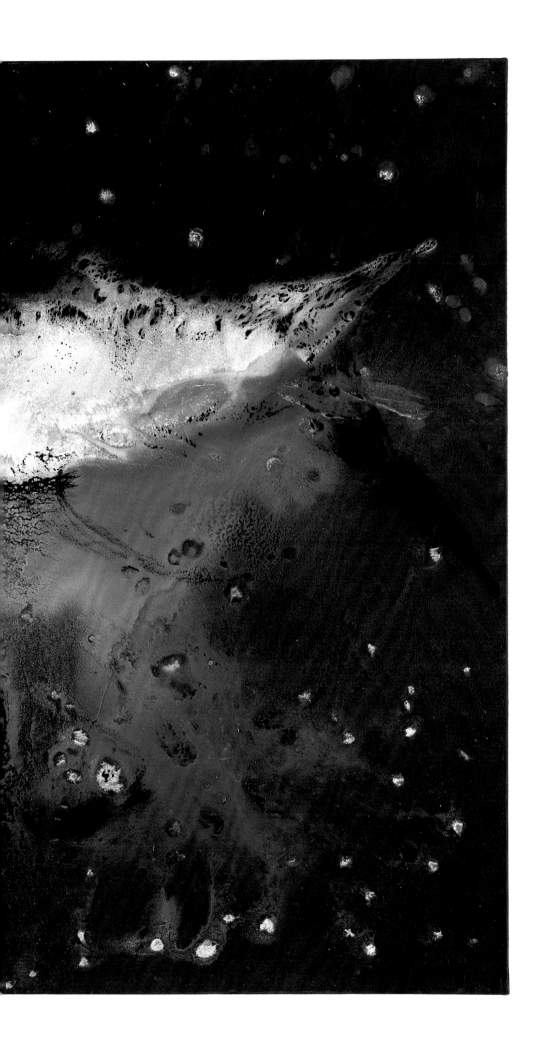

Gran thunnus, 2015
Mixed media on canvas
63 x 94 $^1/_2$ inches (160 x 240 cm)

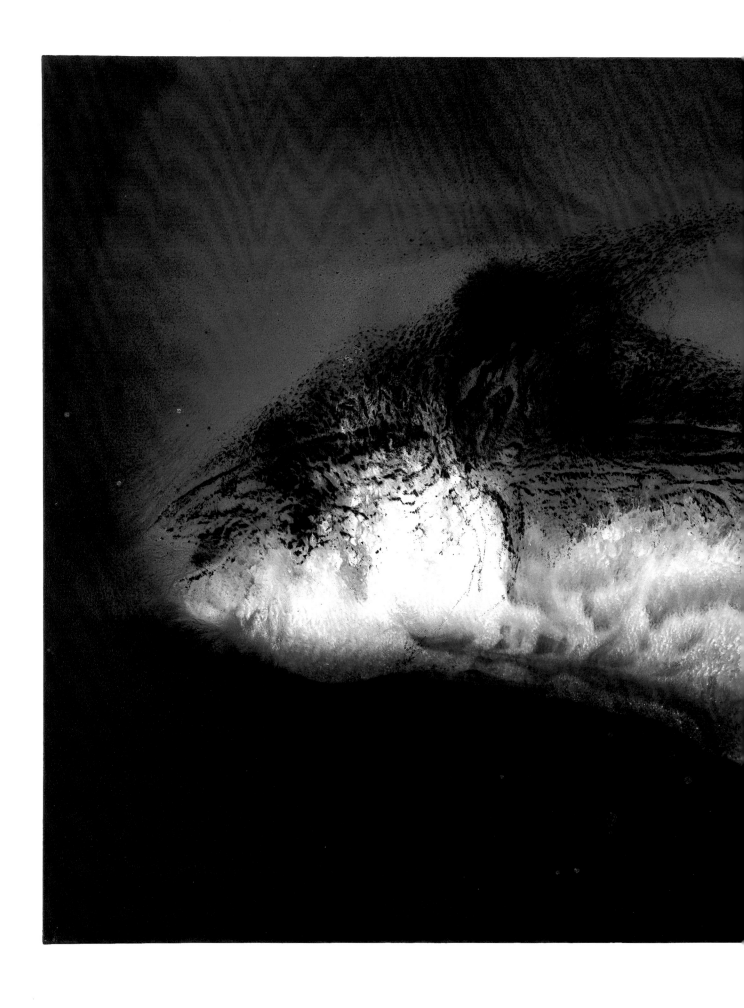

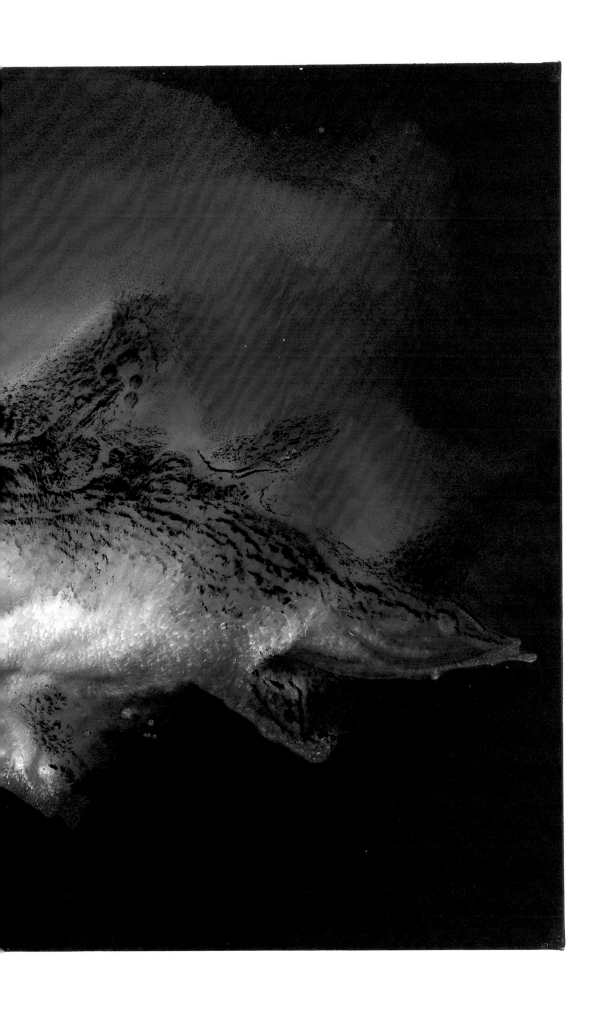

PLATE 11
Peix prècambric, 2015
Mixed media on canvas
63 x 94^1/$_2$ inches (160 x 240 cm)

PLATE 12

Asteroïde, 2016
Mixed media on canvas
31 $^7/_8$ x 39 $^3/_8$ inches (81 x 100 cm)

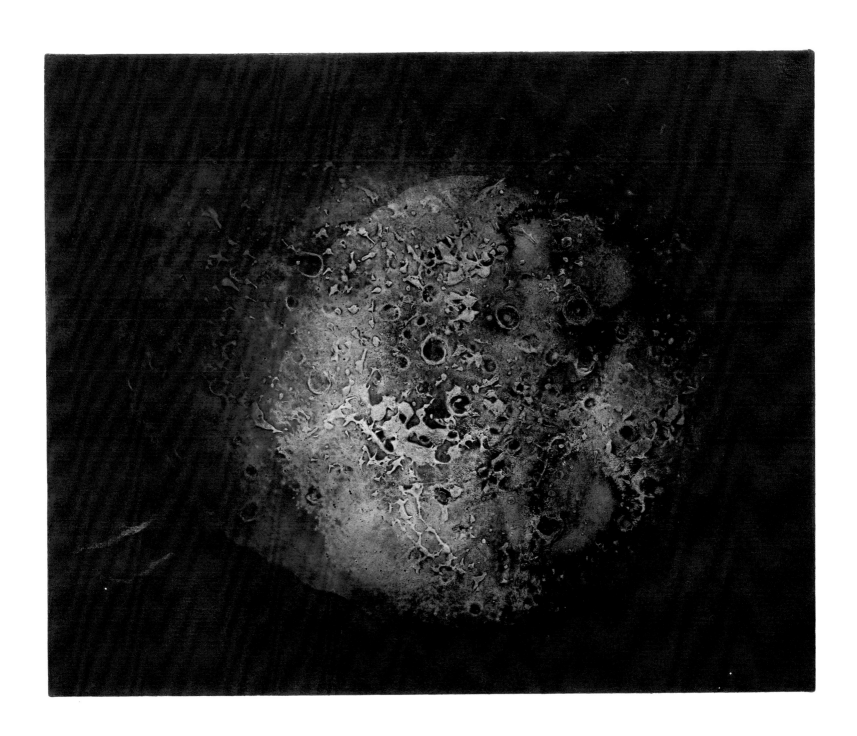

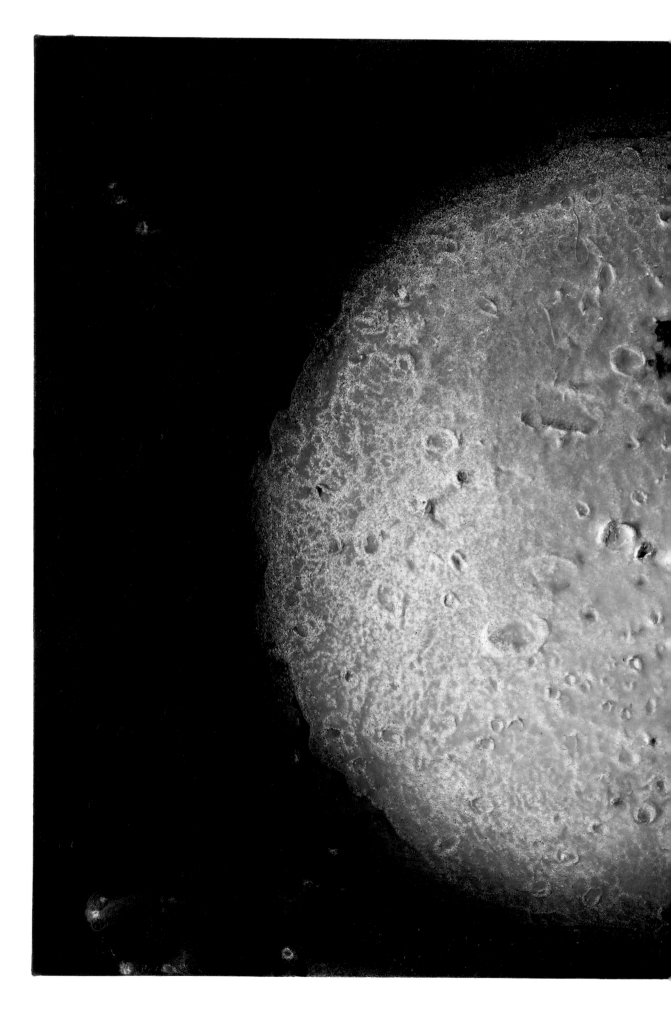

PLATE 13

Llunota, 2015 | Mixed media on canvas | 63 x 94 $^1/_2$ inches (160 x 240 cm)

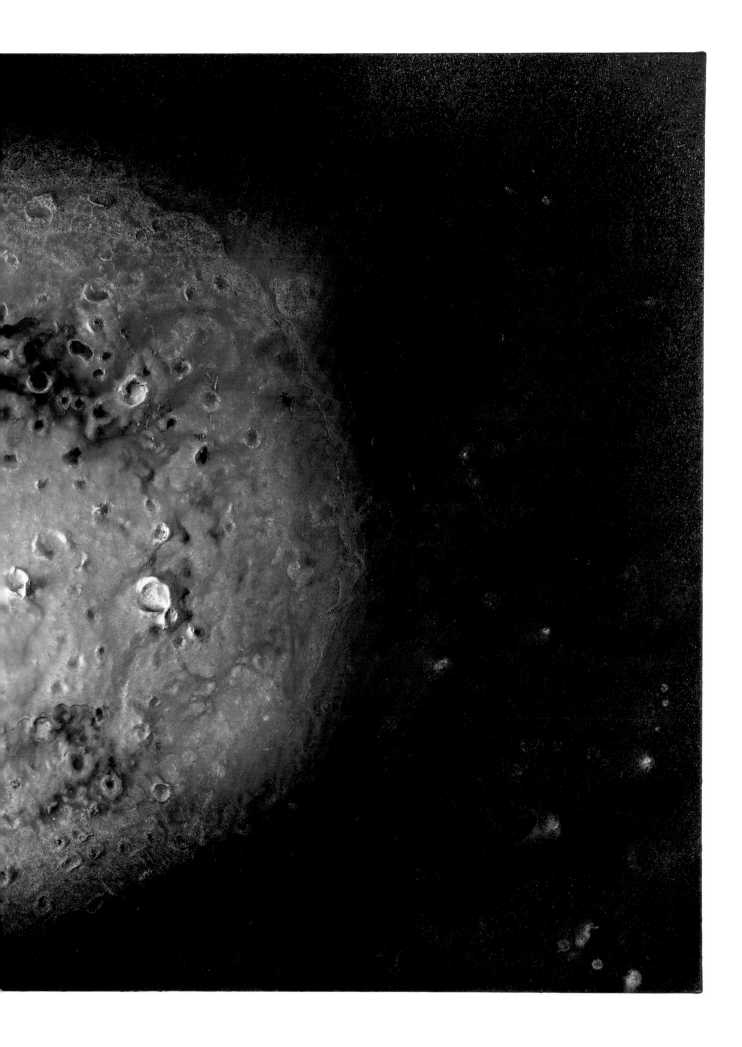

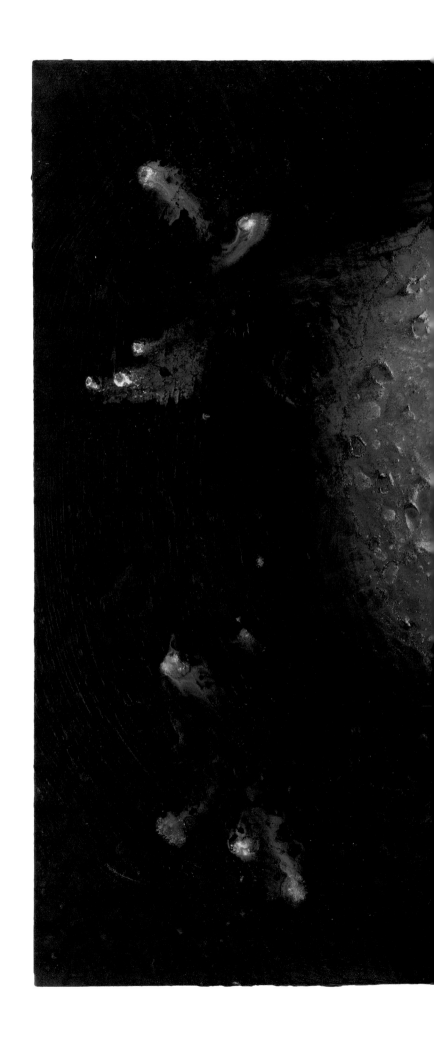

PLATE 14

Exoplanète, 2016
Mixed media on canvas
55 $^1/_2$ x 71 $^1/_4$ inches (141 x 181 cm)

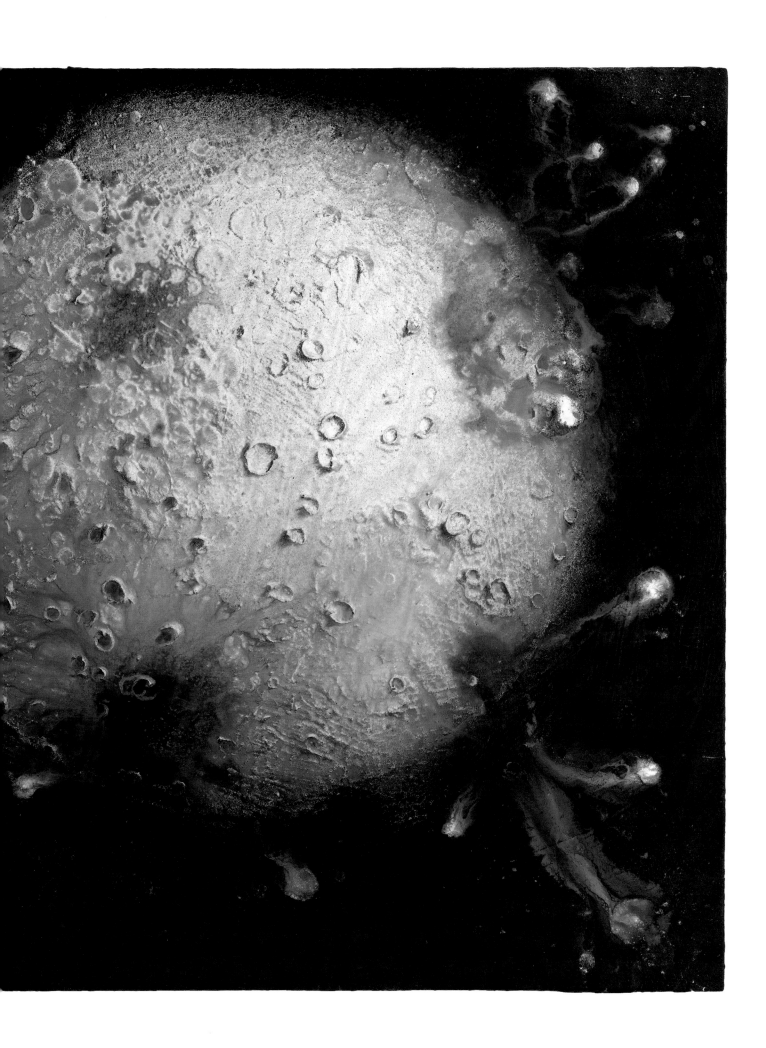

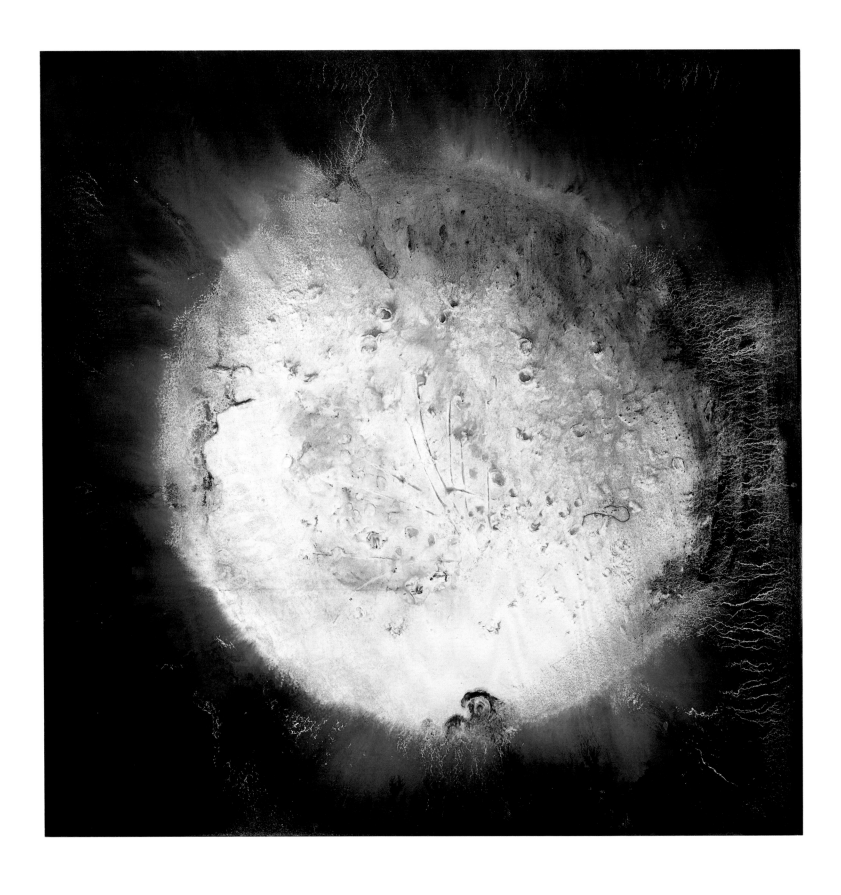

63 $^3/_4$ x 63 $^3/_4$ inches (162 x 162 cm)

PLATE 15

Lune gibbeuse décroissante, 2016
Mixed media on canvas
63 $^3/_4$ x 63 $^3/_4$ inches (162 x 162 cm)

En redondo, April 2016
Mixed media on canvas
45 $^{1}/_{4}$ x 57 $^{1}/_{2}$ inches (115 x 146 cm)

El ruedo, May 2016
Mixed media on canvas
41 $^3/_8$ x 63 $^3/_4$ inches (105 x 162 cm)

Redondos, April 2016
Mixed media on canvas
65 x 67 $^3/_8$ inches (165 x 171 cm)

Primer toro de la tarde, April 2016
Mixed media on canvas
56 $^5/_8$ x 55 $^1/_8$ inches (144 x 140 cm)

PLATE 20

Suerte, June 2016
Mixed media on canvas
33 $^7/_8$ x 41 $^3/_8$ inches (86 x 105 cm)

Cite, June 2016
Mixed media on canvas
46 $^1/_2$ x 82 $^5/_8$ inches (118 x 210 cm)

Esquinero, June 2016
Mixed media on canvas
41 x 55 $^7/_8$ inches (104 x 142 cm)

Albero rosado, June 2016
Mixed media on canvas
65 x 67 inches (165 x 170 cm)

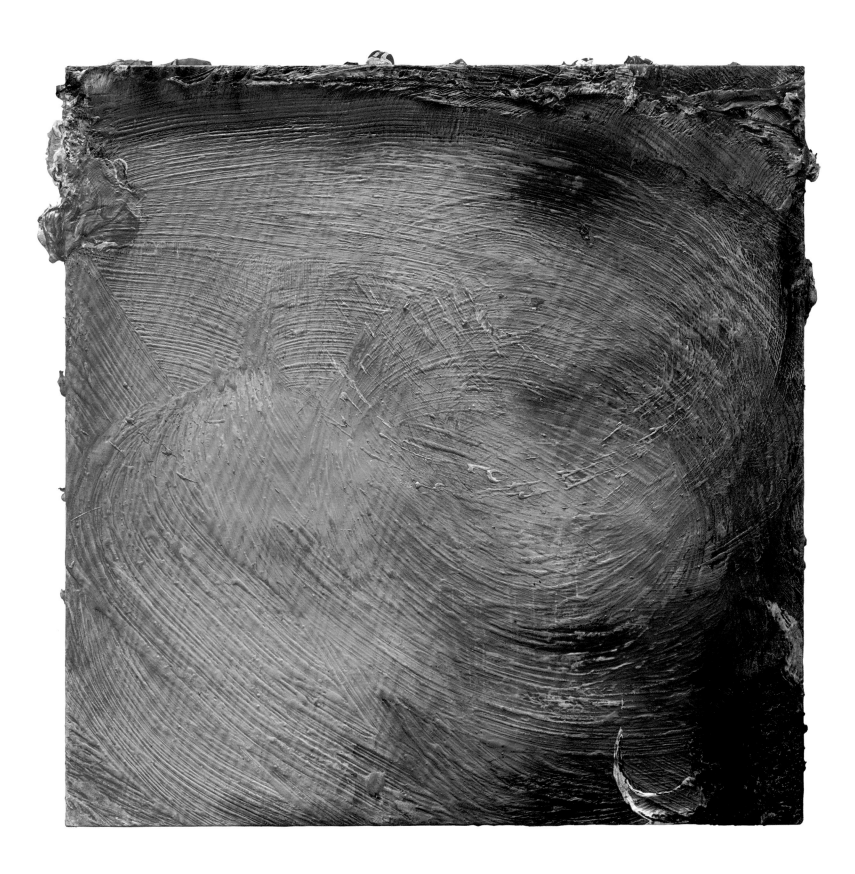

Peixos blancs boca oberta, 2014
Ceramic
17 $^3/_4$ x 9 $^1/_2$ x 9 $^1/_2$ inches (45 x 24 x 24 cm)

34 $^7/_8$ x 19 $^1/_2$ x 12 $^5/_8$ inches (88.5 x 49.5 x 32 cm)

PLATE 25
Ram, 2014
Ceramic
34 $^7/_8$ x 19 $^1/_2$ x 12 $^5/_8$ inches (88.5 x 49.5 x 32 cm)

PLATE 26
Aixencada, 2014
Ceramic
13 $^3/_8$ x 9 $^7/_8$ x 9 $^7/_8$ inches (34 x 25 x 25 cm)

PLATE 27
Cap d'ego, 2014
Ceramic
18 $^{7}/_{8}$ x 12 $^{1}/_{4}$ x 9 inches (48 x 31 x 23 cm)

PLATE 28
Acotada, 2014
Ceramic
15 x 16$^1/_8$ x 13 inches (38 x 41 x 33 cm)

Dorada, 2014
Ceramic
18 $^1/_8$ x 12 $^1/_4$ x 9 $^1/_4$ inches (46 x 31 x 23.5 cm)

PLATE 30
Peix de sorra, 2014
Ceramic
20 x 12 x 10 $^3/_8$ inches (51 x 30.5 x 26.5 cm)

PLATE 31
À casa bianca neve nera, 2014
Ceramic
25 $^1/_4$ x 14 $^5/_8$ x 13 inches (64 x 37 x 33 cm)

Retrat de família, 2014
Ceramic
28 x 48 $^1/_4$ x 17 $^3/_4$ inches (71 x 122.5 x 45 cm)

CHECKLIST

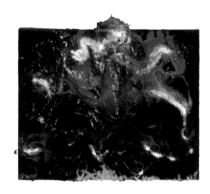

PLATE 1

Little Big Bang, 2014

Mixed media on canvas

23 $^5/_8$ x 31 $^1/_2$ inches (60 x 80 cm)

PLATE 2

Petit cosmos, 2015

Mixed media on canvas

39 $^3/_8$ x 31 $^7/_8$ inches (100 x 81 cm)

PLATE 3

Pop blau, 2015

Mixed media on canvas

32 $^1/_4$ x 36 $^5/_8$ inches (82 x 93 cm)

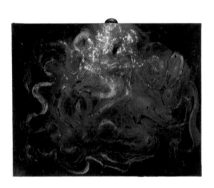

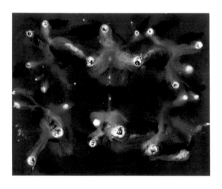

PLATE 4

Pop de fonera, 2015

Mixed media on canvas

33 $^1/_2$ x 41 $^3/_8$ inches (85 x 105 cm)

PLATE 5

Doble CEPH., 2015

Mixed media on canvas

48 $^7/_8$ x 77 $^3/_4$ inches (114 x 195 cm)

PLATE 6

Larvaire, 2015

Mixed media on canvas

74 $^7/_8$ x 94 $^1/_2$ inches (190 x 240 cm)

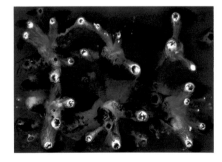

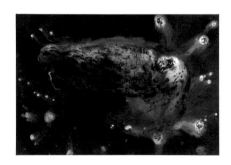

PLATE 7

De·Profundis, 2015

Mixed media on canvas

74 $^3/_4$ x 106 $^1/_4$ inches (190 x 270 cm)

PLATE 8

Kraken central, 2015

Mixed media on canvas

74 $^3/_4$ x 106 $^1/_4$ inches (190 x 270 cm)

PLATE 9

Sipiota, 2015

Mixed media on canvas

51 $^1/_8$ x 77 $^3/_4$ inches (130 x 195 cm)

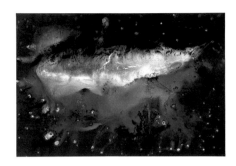

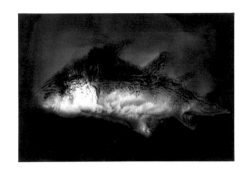

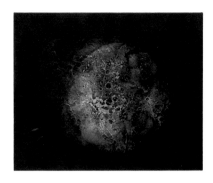

PLATE 10

Gran thunnus, 2015

Mixed media on canvas

63 x 94 ^{1}/2 inches (160 x 240 cm)

PLATE 11

Peix prècambric, 2015

Mixed media on canvas

63 x 94 ^{1}/2 inches (160 x 240 cm)

PLATE 12

Asteroïde, 2016

Mixed media on canvas

31 ^{7}/8 x 39 ^{3}/8 inches (81 x 100 cm)

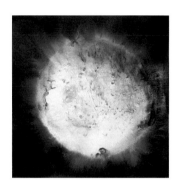

PLATE 13

Llunota, 2015

Mixed media on canvas

63 x 94 ^{1}/2 inches (160 x 240 cm)

PLATE 14

Exoplanète, 2016

Mixed media on canvas

55 ^{1}/2 x 71 ^{1}/4 inches (141 x 181 cm)

PLATE 15

Lune gibbeuse décroissante, 2016

Mixed media on canvas

63 ^{3}/4 x 63 ^{3}/4 inches (162 x 162 cm)

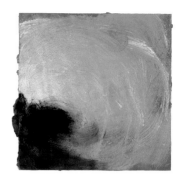

PLATE 16

En redondo, April 2016

Mixed media on canvas

45 $^1/_4$ x 57 $^1/_2$ inches (115 x 146 cm)

PLATE 17

El ruedo, May 2016

Mixed media on canvas

41 $^3/_8$ x 63 $^3/_4$ inches (105 x 162 cm)

PLATE 18

Redondos, April 2016

Mixed media on canvas

65 x 67 $^3/_8$ inches (165 x 171 cm)

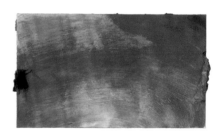

PLATE 19

Primer toro de la tarde, April 2016

Mixed media on canvas

56 $^5/_8$ x 55 $^1/_8$ inches (144 x 140 cm)

PLATE 20

Suerte, June 2016

Mixed media on canvas

33 $^7/_8$ x 41 $^3/_8$ inches (86 x 105 cm)

PLATE 21

Cite, June 2016

Mixed media on canvas

46 $^1/_2$ x 82 $^5/_8$ inches (118 x 210 cm)

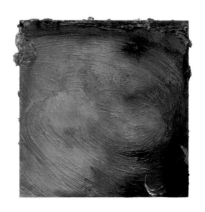

PLATE 22

Esquinero, June 2016

Mixed media on canvas

41 x 55 $^7/_8$ inches (104 x 142 cm)

PLATE 23

Albero rosado, June 2016

Mixed media on canvas

65 x 67 inches (165 x 170 cm)

PLATE 24

Peixos blancs boca oberta, 2014
Ceramic
17 3/4 x 9 1/2 x 9 1/2 inches (45 x 24 x 24 cm)

PLATE 25

Ram, 2014
Ceramic
34 7/8 x 19 1/2 x 12 5/8 inches (88.5 x 49.5 x 32 cm)

PLATE 26

Aixencada, 2014
Ceramic
13 3/8 x 9 7/8 x 9 7/8 inches (34 x 25 x 25 cm)

PLATE 27

Cap d'ego, 2014
Ceramic
18 7/8 x 12 1/4 x 9 inches (48 x 31 x 23 cm)

PLATE 28

Acotada, 2014
Ceramic
15 x 16 1/8 x 13 inches (38 x 41 x 33 cm)

PLATE 29

Dorada, 2014
Ceramic
18 1/8 x 12 1/4 x 9 1/4 inches (46 x 31 x 23.5 cm)

PLATE 30

Peix de sorra, 2014
Ceramic
20 x 12 x 10 3/8 inches (51 x 30.5 x 26.5 cm)

PLATE 31

À casa bianca neve nera, 2014
Ceramic
25 1/4 x 14 5/8 x 13 inches (64 x 37 x 33 cm)

PLATE 32

Retrat de família, 2014
Ceramic
28 x 48 1/4 x 17 3/4 inches (71 x 122.5 x 45 cm)

EXHIBITION HISTORY

SELECTED EXHIBITIONS

1974

Galería d'Art Picarol, Cala d'Or, *Barceló Artigues*,
September 13-October 15, 1974.

1976

Galería 4 Gats, Palma de Mallorca, *Barceló Artigues*,
February 9-25, 1976.

Museo Mallorca, Palma de Mallorca, *Cadaverina 15*,
November 8-23, 1976.

1977

Galería 4 Gats, Palma, *Miquel Barceló Artigues*,
April 25-May 14,1977.

1978

Galería Sa Pleta Freda, Son Servera, *Miquel Barceló Artigues*,
March 18-April 15, 1978.

1981

Galería Metronom, Barcelona, *Llibres Pintats*,
February 19-26, 1981.

1982

Colegio de Arquitectos, Palma de Mallorca, *Miquel Barceló*,
February-March 1982.

Galería Fúcares, Almagro, *Miquel Barceló. Pinturas*,
May 22-June 25, 1982.

Galería Trece, Barcelona, *Barceló*,
April 20-May 15, 1982.

Galerie Axe Art Actuel, Toulouse,
December 14 1982-January 15, 1983.

1983

Galerie Med a Mothi, Montpellier, *Pintagossos*,
March 4-25,1983.

Galleria Lucio Amelio, Naples, *Miquel Barceló*,
June-July 1983.

Galerie Yvon Lambert, Paris, *Miquel Barceló*,
December 1983-January 1984.

1984

Galerie Bruno Bischofberger, Zurich, *Miquel Barceló*,
June 12-July 14, 1984.

Galería Juana de Aizpuru, Madrid, *Miquel Barceló*,
November 30, 1984-January 20, 1985.

1985

Akira Ikeda Gallery, Nagoya, *Miquel Barceló. New Painting*,
January 7-31,1985.

Galerie Rudolf Zwirner, Cologne, *Miquel Barceló neue arbeiten*,
April 26-May 1985.

CAPC, Bordeaux, *Miquel Barceló. Peintures de 1983 à 1985*,
May 10 - September 8, 1985.

This exhibition traveled to:

Palacio de Velázquez, Madrid,
September 14-October 13, 1985.

And to:

Institute of Contemporary Art, Boston,
February 18-April 20, 1986.

Anders Torngerg Gallery, Lund, *Miquel Barceló.
Drawings 1985*,
October 4-29, 1985.

Galerie Bruno Bischofberger, Zurich, *Miquel Barceló.
Neue Bilder*,
November 23-December 21, 1985.

1986

Thomas Segal Gallery, Boston,
January 11-February 22, 1986.

Institute of Contemporary Art, Boston.
Miquel Barceló. Peintures de 1983 à 1985.
February 18-April 20, 1986.

Leo Castelli Gallery, New York,
April-May 1986.

Anders Tornberg Gallery, Stockholm, *Miquel Barceló.
Drawings 1985*,
October 4-29, 1986.

1987

Galerie Yvon Lambert, Paris, *Miquel Barceló*,
February 21-March 17, 1987.

Galerie Michael Haas, Berlin, *Miquel Barceló*,
March 13-April 18, 1987.

Waddington Galleries, London, *Miquel Barceló*,
April 29-May 22, 1987.

L'Antic Teatre de la Casa de la Caritat, Barcelona,
*Barceló - Barcelona. Miquel Barceló. Pintura
de 1985 a 1987*,
November 27, 1987-January 24, 1988.

1988

Galerie Bruno Bischofberger, Zurich.

Musée d'Art Contemporain de Montreal, Montreal,
Miquel Barceló: Peintures récentes,
    February 28-May 22, 1988.

1989
Galleria Lucio Amelio, Naples, *Miquel Barceló*,
    February 18-March 1989.

Galeria Dau al Set, Barcelona, *Barceló in Mali*,
    May 12-June 1989.

Leo Castelli Gallery, New York, *Paintings*,
    November 1989.

Castelli Graphics, New York, *Drawings and Prints*,
    November 1989.

1990
Galería Soledad Lorenzo, Madrid, *Miquel Barceló*,
    January 25-February 24, 1990.

Waddington Galleries, London, *Miquel Barceló*,
    February 28-March 24, 1990.

Manel Mayoral Galeria d'Art, Barcelona, *Miquel Barceló*,
    May 1990.

Galerie Yvon Lambert, Paris, *Miquel Barceló*,
    September 8-October 10, 1990.

1991
Galerie Bruno Bischofberger, Zurich, *Toros*,
    June 6-July 20, 1991.

Musée d'Art Contemporain de Nimes, Nimes, *Miquel Barceló*,
    July 5-September 30, 1991.

1992
Galería Soledad Lorenzo, Madrid, *Miquel Barceló*,
    January 30-March 7, 1992.

First Gallery, Moscow, *Miquel Barceló*,
    March-April 1992.

Piece Unique, Paris, *Miquel Barceló*,
    April-May 1992.

Galería Salvador Riera, Barcelona, *Miquel Barceló*,
    June 11-August 1992.

Gana Art Gallery, Seoul, *Miquel Barceló*,
    October 1-10, 1992.

Leo Castelli Gallery, New York, *De Rerum Natura*,
    1992.

1993
Galerie Bruno Bischofberger, Zurich, *Miquel Barceló.
New Works*,
    April-June 1993.

Galeria Nasoni, Lisbon, *Miquel Barceló*,
    April 30-May 1993.

    This exhibition traveled to:

Galeria Nasoni, Porto,
    May 20-June 1993.

Galleria Civica di Arte Contemporanea, Trento, *Barceló*,
    May 22-July 11, 1993.

Kunsthal Rotterdam, Rotterdam, *Miquel Barceló:
Tekeningen van Mali*,
    August 28-October 10, 1993.

1994
Galería Soledad Lorenzo, Madrid, *Miquel Barceló*,
    January 25-February 26, 1994.

Galerie Bruno Bischofberger, Zurich, *Miquel Barceló. Portraits*,
    June 10-September 9, 1994Whitechapel Art Gallery, London,

Miquel Barceló: 1984-1994,
    September 23-November 20. 1994.

    This exhibition traveled to:

Centre del Carmen, Valencia,
    January 26-April 23, 1995.

Galerie Kyoto Chirathivat, Bangkok, *Miquel Barceló*,
    December 7, 1994-February 19,1995.

1995
Leo Castelli Gallery, New York, *Miquel Barceló*,
    April 29-May 20, 1995.

1996
Galerie Lucie Weill Seligmann, Paris, *Estampes*,
    March 5-April 1996.

Galerie d'art graphique du Musée National d'Art Moderne du Centre
National d'Art et Culture George Pompidou, Paris, *Miquel Barceló:
Impressions d'Afrique*,
    March 6-April 29, 1996.

Galerie Nationale du Jeu de Paume, Paris, Miquel Barceló,
    March 5-May 1996.

1997
Museum voor Moderne Kunst, Ostende, *Miquel Barceló. Stillevens*,
    April 25-June 1, 1997.

Château de Chenonceau, Chenonceaux, *Miquel Barceló*,
    May 31-November 3, 1997.

Sala Cronopios, Centro Cultural Recoleta, Buenos Aires,
Miquel Barceló,
    November 6-December 14, 1997.

1997 (continued)
Galería Soledad Lorenzo, Madrid, *Miquel Barceló.*
Obra 1996-1997,
    November 27–December 31, 1997.

1998
Timothy Taylor Gallery, London, *Miquel Barceló,*
    March 18–April 25, 1998.

Museu d'Art Contemporani de Barcelona (Macba), Barcelona,
Miquel Barceló: 1987-1997,
    April 2–June 21, 1998.

Iglesia Santa Eulalia dei Catalani, Festival Sul Novecento, Palermo,
Il Cristo della Vucciria. Pinturas y cerámicas,
    October 17 – December 13, 1998.

Centro Permanente de Exposiciones del Monasterio Santo Domingo
de Silos, Burgos, (on the occasion of the inauguration of the
exhibition halls).

1999
Museo de Bellas Artes, Oviedo, *Des citrons coupés,*
    February 1999.

Museu d'Art Contemporani - Fundació Juan March, Palma,
Miquel Barceló,
    June 22–October 1999.

    This exhibition traveled to:

Museu de la Ceràmica, Barcelona,
    February–July 2000.

Museo Nacional Centro de Arte Reina Sofía, Madrid, *Miquel Barceló,*
Obra sobre papel 1979-1999,
    September 14–November 21, 1999.

    This exhibiton traveled to:

Sala La General, Granada,
    December 1999–January 2000;

Museu de Arte, São Paulo, Brazil,
    March–April, 2000;

    and to:

Museo de Arte Moderno, Montevideo, Uruguay,
    June–July 2000;

    and to:

Tel Aviv Museum of Art,
    October–December 2000.

Fons Documental Miquel Barceló, Artà, *El llibre per*
a cecs de Miquel Barceló,
    August–October 1999.

2000
Grant Selwyn Fine Art, New York, *Miquel Barceló,*
    April 12–June 17, 2000.

Fons Documental Miquel Barceló, Artà, *Miquel Barceló i*
Manuel de Falla,
    August 6–September 15, 2000.

Musée des arts décoratifs, Paris, *Miquel Barceló, un*
peintre et la céramique,
    November 27–December 12, 2000.

2001
Jablonka Galerie, Cologne, *Miquel Barceló, L'ours blessé,*
    April 27–May 26, 2001.

Timothy Taylor Gallery, London, *Miquel Barceló, new*
paintings and ceramics,
    June 22–August 18, 2001.

Fons Documental Miquel Barceló, Artà, *La Cuina de*
Miquel Barceló,
    August 5–September 30, 2001.

Pabellon de "Sociedad Anónima Tudela Veguin" Feria
Internacional de Muestras de Asturias, *Miquel Barceló,*
    August 4–19, 2001.

2002
Galleria Paolo Curti & Co, Milan, *Barceló. Raccolta di Polvere,*
    March 12–April 30, 2002.

Fondation Maeght, Saint-Paul de Vence, *Miquel Barceló. Mapamundi,*
    April 12–June 20, 2002.

Abadía de Santo Domingo de Silos, Silos, *Miquel Barceló en Silos,*
    May 20–July 15, 2002.

Fons Documental Miquel Barceló, Artà, *La Biblioteca de*
Miquel Barceló,
    August–October 2002.

Galleria Nazionale d'Arte Moderna, Rome, *L'Atelier di Miquel Barceló,*
    September 2002–January 2003.

2003
La llotja, Palma; Museu de Menorca, Maó; Capella del Roser, Ciutadella
de Menorca; Museu d'Art Contemporani d'Eivissa, Eivissa.; Plaça de
Francesc Xavier, Formentera. *Miquel Barceló a les Illes Balears,*
    April 29–August 31, 2003.

Fundación Museo del Grabado Español Contemporáneo, Marbella,
Miquel Barceló,
    July 18–September 13, 2003.

Antigua Plaza del Pescado, Oviedo, *Miquel Barceló. Obras de*
la Colección Masaveu,
    October 2003.

Pinacoteca do Estado, São Paulo, *Barceló*,
December 13, 2003-February 22, 2004.

This exhibition traveled to:

Museum August Kestner, Hannover,
September 23-November 7, 2004;

MARCO-Museo de Arte Contemporáneo de Monterrey, Monterrey,
February-April 2005;

and to:

Museo Rufino Tamayo, Mexico City,
May 12-July 31, 2005.

2004
Galleria Paolo Curti & Co, Milan, *Miquel Barceló. Sculture*,
March 9-April 30, 2004.

Salle d'actualité du département des Arts graphiques. Musée du
Louvre, Paris, *La Divine Comédie. Dessins de Miquel Barceló*,
April 9-July 5, 2004.

Sala de exposiciones "Ignacio Zuloaga" y Museo del Grabado,
Fuendetodos, *Miquel Barceló*,
June 19-September 19, 2004.

Museo de las artes de la Universidad de Guadalajara, Guadalajara,
Miquel Barceló, La Divina Comedia,
November 27, 2004-January 30, 2005.

2005
C & M Arts, New York, *Miquel Barceló*,
January 25-March 5, 2005.

Galerie Bruno Bischofberger, Zurich, *Miquel Barceló.
New Works*,
March 17-April 23, 2005.

Sala Kubo, San Sebastián, *Las formas del mundo*,
May 4-July 17, 2005.

Arteko Galería, San Sebastián, *Barceló. Obra Gráfica.
Serie Lanzarote*,
May 5-June 2005.

Castel Nuovo Maschio Angionio, Naples, *Miquel Barceló.
La Divina Comedia*,
October 10-November 20, 2005.

Galería Gacma, Málaga, *Gesto de la naturaleza. Miquel Barceló*,
December 2, 2005-February 2, 2006.

2006
Timothy Taylor Gallery, London, *Miquel Barceló:
New Etchings*,
January 9-February 4, 2006.

Église des Célestins, 60º Festival d'Avignon, Avignon,
*Miquel Barceló, Exposition. Sculptures, Céramiques et
Dessins au fusain*,
July 8-27, 2006.

Jablonka Galerie, Cologne, *Miquel Barceló.
Cerámicas / Ceramics*,
May 19-August 15, 2006.

Museo d'Arte Moderna, Lugano, *Miquel Barceló*,
November 12, 2006-February 4, 2007.

Centro Cultural Fundación Círculo de Lectores, Barcelona,
Miquel Barceló la Divina Commedia,
December 12, 2006-February 28, 2007.

2007
Galerie Yvon Lambert, Paris, *Miquel Barceló*,
April 21-May 26, 2007.

LongHouse Reserve, New York, *Miquel Barceló Clay
and Bronze*,
July 27-October 6, 2007.

Fundación Francisco Godia, Barcelona, *Barceló en
las colecciones privadas de Barcelona*,
October 23, 2007-January 6, 2008.

2008
Irish Museum of Modern Art, Dublin, *Miquel Barceló: The
African Work*,
June 25-September 28, 2008.

This exhibition traveled to:

CAC Centro de Arte Contemporáneo de Málaga,
Miquel Barceló: Obra africana,
November 11, 2008-February 15, 2009.

Pilar Corrias Gallery, London, *Miquel Barceló. Cephalopod Works*,
November 25, 2008-January 10, 2009.

2009
Spanish Pavillion, 53rd International Art Exhibition,
Venice Biennale, *Miquel Barceló*,
June 7-November 22, 2009.

Fundació Pilar i Joan Miró a Mallorca, Palma, *Barceló abans
de Barceló 1973-1982*,
June 24-September 27, 2009.

This exhibition traveled to:

Les Abattoirs. Musée d'Art Moderne et Contemporain, Toulouse,
November 20, 2009-February 28, 2010;

and to:

Arts Santa Mònica, Barcelona,
July 15-September 26, 2010

2009 (continued)
Galerie Bruno Bischofberger, Zurich, *Miquel Barceló.*
Recent Works,
   May 23–July 24, 2009.

2010
Caixa Forum, Madrid, *Miquel Barceló. La solitude*
organisative. 1983-2009,
   February 11–June 13, 2010.

   This exhibition traveled to:

Caixa Forum, Barcelona,
   July 16, 2010–January 9, 2011

Palais des Papes, Petit Palais, Collection Lambert, Avignon,
Terramare Miquel Barceló,
   June 27–November 7, 2010.

2011
Ben Brown Fine Arts, Hong Kong, Miquel Barceló. *Recent*
paintings, ceramics and sculpture,
   May 24–July 29, 2011.

Théâtre des Bouffes du Nord, Paris, *Le taj. Peinture en scène,*
   October 18–28, 2011.

Lisbon and Estoril Film Festival, Torre de Bélem, Lisbon,
Miquel Barceló. Work in progress,
   November 9–18, 2011

Marlborough Gallery, the Union Square Partnership and the City of
New York's Department of Parks & Recreation Public Art Program,
New York, *Miquel Barceló: Elefandret Sculpture at Union Square,*
   September 3, 2011–May 29, 2012.

2012
Museu d'Art Contemporani d'Eivissa, Ibiza, *Barry Flanagan i*
Miquel Barceló: Ceràmiques i obra sobre paper,
   April 27–October 31, 2012.

Galerie Bruno Bischofberger, Zurich, *Miquel Barceló – Ceramics,*
   December 3, 2012–April 5, 2013.

Bank Austria Kunstforum, Vienna, *Miquel Barceló,*
   December 12, 2012–March 10, 2013.

2013
Galería Elvira González, Madrid, *Miquel Barceló,*
   January 26, 2013–March 27, 2013.

Musée d'Art Moderne de Céret, Céret, *Terra Ignis Miquel Barceló,*
   June 29–November 12, 2013.

   This exhibition traveled to:

Museu Nacional do Azulejo, Lisbon,
   September 24–November 24, 2013.

Acquavella Galleries, New York, *Miquel Barceló,*
   October 9–November 22, 2013.

2014
Ben Brown Fine Arts, Hong Kong, *Miquel Barceló: Courant Central,*
   May 14–July 15, 2014.

Pinakotheke, Sao Paulo, *Miquel Barceló. Pinturas,*
Esculturas y Cerámica,
   May 20–July 12, 2014.

   This exhibition traveled to:

Pinakotheke, Rio de Janeiro,
   September 23–August 30, 2014;

Galeria Multiarte, Fortaleza,
   November 11–December 15, 2014.

2015
Galerie Thaddaeus Ropac, Paris, *Miquel Barceló. L'Inassèchement,*
   April 25–May 31, 2015.

Galerie Bruno Bischofberger AG, Maennedorf, *Miquel Barceló.*
Ardenti Germinat. New Paintings and Works on Paper,
   October 2–November 27, 2015.

Calcografía Nacional, Madrid, Miquel Barceló. Gráfico,
   November 19, 2015–January 20, 2016.

2016
Musée national Picasso-Paris, *Miquel Barceló. Sol y sombra*
   March 22–September 30, 2016

   and at:

BnF I François-Mitterand
   March 22–August 28, 2016.

Poster designed by Miquel Barceló
for the Nimes bullfighting festival in 1988

Poster designed by Miquel Barceló for a bullfight on
September 4, 2016 to honor the torero Victor Barrios, who was killed
in the bullring in the town of Teruel in July 2016.